Against the Wind: You've Got the Power

Rosita Hall

ROSITA HALL

AGAINST THE WIND

YOU'VE GOT THE POWER

Epic Press

Belleville, Ontario, Canada

ISBN: 978-1-4600-0108-0
LSI Edition: 978-1-4600-0109-7
E-book ISBN: 978-1-4600-0110-3
(E-book available from the Kindle Store, KOBO and the iBookstore)

Cataloguing data available from Library and Archives Canada

To order additional copies, visit:
www.essencebookstore.com

For more information, please contact:
www.rositahall.com
905-385-4613

Epic Press is an imprint of *Essence Publishing,* a Christian Book Publisher dedicated to furthering the work of Christ through the written word. For more information, contact:
20 Hanna Court, Belleville, Ontario, Canada K8P 5J2
Phone: 1-800-238-6376 • Fax: (613) 962-3055
Email: info@essence-publishing.com
Web site: www.essence-publishing.com

Printed in Canada
by

E**p**ic
Press

DEDICATION

To Josh and Chris—two of the finest young men a mother could ever ask for.

I have reserved a spot for two in a special corner of my heart—and it says RESERVED—VIP, and that spot can never be filled by anyone else or anything else. I am blessed beyond my wildest imagination. Thank you both for showering me daily with love and laughter! I am so proud of you both.

And last but not least, to my husband Norm. I had someone recently ask if I read love stories, and I replied, "I don't need to read love stories because my life with Norm is a love story, and it has been for thirty years." Thank you, Norm, for your daily love, respect, encouragement, and laughter.

Contents

Foreword
To Daddy...Against the Wind

I remember as a teenager driving in the car with my daddy one afternoon, and the radio was playing "Against the Wind," by Bob Seger and the Silver Bullet Band. My dad was singing along, and while the song had a nice jingle, I had no idea what it was about (and still don't), but I kept joining in at the chorus because it had such a nice little beat to it. "Against the wind, we were runnin' against the wind, we were young and strong, we were runnin' against the wind...."

Suddenly my dad stopped singing, looked over at me, and said, "Rosie, in this life you must never run against the wind—run with the wind because it is a lot easier." I remember that day like it was yesterday.

For a while, in my younger years I heeded his advice. But as the years moved on and life happened at such a quick pace and opportunities unveiled themselves to me, I realized that running with the wind was not always the best option. Sometimes you have to take a chance and run against the wind—sometimes it's the opposition that gives us the greatest opportunity.

A kite rises *against* the wind, not *with* the wind. It's the opposition that allows the kite to rise. Opposition has enabled me to feast on some of my greatest successes. And like the kite reaching its greatest height against the wind, I too have done the same. So here's to my daddy (may his soul rest in peace)—your incredible advice was part of the wisdom I needed during the earlier part of my journey, but as the roads began to widen and I became wiser, I realized that I had the power to run against the wind as well. So be proud of me, Daddy, because as the song goes "I'm older now and seeking shelter against the wind," and that fierce boldness has afforded me many blessings, great family and friends, and incredible business success!

And so now as I sit here listening to that old Bob Seger song, reminiscing about that time with my daddy—I realize that I now have some advice to pass on to my two sons, Joshua and Christian, and it is simply this: go boldly and fiercely as you journey through this beautiful life and *run against the wind!* Opportunities await you both! *You've got the power!*

Finally:
The Power of the Journey

Finally I am ready for the journey. I do not know which way the roads will lead, but I know unequivocally that there is a purpose for the journey and for my existence. My life has been carefully designed. My mission has been deliberately etched in the depths of my heart and soul and can only be revealed by the one who created me. His truth becomes my guiding light. I am sometimes distracted along the way, and I sinfully engage in the desires of my ego, but quickly the symphony in my heart beckons me back to the path of my soul's yearning. Discernment echoes to me to stay the course and reminds me that the path is filled with boundless possibilities that stretch beyond what my mind can conceive.

I am intrigued by the miracles along the way, fascinated by the unexpected, grieved by wars, hatred, violence, and losses. I am awakened by the truths about myself and others, energized by the forces of life, protected by grace, and inspired by the hope I see through the eyes of my children. I hunger to continue the journey.

Each day I feast upon its delicious intangible opportunities. On one particular day, I feel this incredible force within me: so much strength, wisdom, and confidence that I am a little overwhelmed. And then it happens: I have an "aha moment," and in unison with that moment, my heart opens and receives the gift of life. Now for the first time, I can taste the delicious flavour of goodness and a presence much bigger than I. His grace has found me. I feast upon it and continue to do so every moment of each day. I have arrived at a critical place on the journey—but the journey has only just begun!

As you continue on your journey, may the pages to follow provide you with practical tips and remind you that *You've Got the Power* to deal with the daily stressors, changes, and challenges you will experience both on and off the job! Enjoy!

Rosita Hall
2006-01-17

The Power to Connect Within

*"You cannot hide from yourself—
there is no space big enough."* –Rosita

HEY SOUL SISTERS...

A woman gazes in the mirror at the age of fifty-two; she sees more than one reflection staring back. She is in awe of their commanding presence...what an astounding moment. Each face beckons her to a different place and time in her life. For a moment she thinks she's dreaming, but the reality is so vivid and powerful that she knows she is truly awake and experiencing something incredible. Beneath her laugh lines, aging skin, and those expressive eyes she sees reflections of herself—the young girl she once was, the young woman she was at twenty or so, the middle-aged woman she is now, and an old woman. Each one connected by a common thread called sisterhood.

The young girl she once was smiles with her youthful spirit, playfulness, and innocence. The woman realizes she has not lost this God-given gift, as it is fully alive. This young energy is her constant reminder to laugh out loud, not to take herself too seriously, and to keep a youthful perspective. The young girl's spirit is sheer joy and fun wrapped in an abundance of love and excitement. But the young girl is also a reminder that childhood can only be lived once, but a youthful heart lives on forever! The woman embraces this and then whispers to herself, "I will never let go of my youthful heart and spirit!"

As the woman stares deeper into the mirror, her youthful spirit fades and suddenly, as if someone has hit the fast-forward button, she finds herself face to face with a young woman about the age of twenty-four. The young woman smiles. She displays her matured authentic grace and truth. Her radiance tells the unwritten story of a young woman who clearly took advantage of the delicious opportunities that surrounded her in abundance; she cautiously feasted upon those she could afford to digest emotionally, mentally, physically, and spiritually.

She has made many mistakes along the way, but she knows that each one was sprinkled with life lessons and self-awareness—tools she would need as she continued on the journey. She has fallen completely in love with life. Her physical beauty comes into to full view, and then she fades away....

Suddenly the fifty-two-year-old middle-aged woman sees her own image come back into full view. Her reflection takes up the entire mirror. She is boisterous, full of confidence and poise, a force to be reckoned with. She has overcome many changes, challenges, and adversities. Somewhere buried deep between the crevices of her age lines, she sees traces of joy, sadness, hope, triumph, and fear, but she has travelled each valley and climbed each mountain with dignity and grace. She knows where her strengths lie, and she uses them respectfully to ensure that they don't become her weaknesses. She recognizes her strengths as gifts from God.

As she stares at her reflection once again, her face almost pressed against the mirror, she begins to digest the truth of the woman she has become today. But within seconds, like magic, her image disappears from the mirror and she sees an old woman (with all of her physical attributes) sitting quietly on the sidelines watching and observing. The old woman knows that her future and the condition of her heart and soul are in the hands of, and have been sculpted by, her younger soul sisters.

The fifty-two-year-old woman pauses—each of the reflections playing over and over in her mind. What a powerful connection between each of those images. She is proud of her soul sisters and realizes how each one has impacted her life in such a significant way and how intimately they are intertwined.

Do you recognize your soul sisters? Remember, they are the sculptors who have been shaping and will continue to shape our lives. In particular, they will determine what the old woman will see and how she will live out her golden years. From the moment we are born and into our adult lives we are being shaped by such influence as our parents, siblings, teachers, circumstances, our gender, strangers, and the list goes on and on. The impact of that shaping will influence our emotional, mental, physical, spiritual, and financial reality, as well as how we view the world and ourselves as women. Each of us women has soul sisters living within us—we can never escape them because they are all a part of us. We must remember, however, that once we reach a certain age, we have the power to choose which aspects of our soul sisters we want to continue to take on the journey.

Let's face it, some of us carry heavy burdens and there are certain aspects of our lives we'd rather forget.

But let us first acknowledge *what is* and then make the decision to create the kind of life that will allow us to feel joy, create fulfillment, and live our potential in a way that impacts those around us in a powerful way. We must recognize and examine the impact and then choose carefully those emotional, physical, and spiritual realities we wish to accompany us on the journey.

Take care of your soul sisters along life's way because they will be the driving force behind the life that you live. And one day when that fifty-two-year-old woman looks in the mirror at the ripe old age of eighty or so, she can say, "Hey Soul Sisters—I'm enjoying the ride!"

The Power of WRM Intentions

"Let my daily actions be the answer to someone else's prayer."
—Rosita

Each day when we awaken to the dawn of a new morning, I think we should pause upon arising, give thanks, and then write down what I call our "What Really Matters" (WRM) intentions. I would suggest that you start with just three. WRM intentions are specific and personal intentions that can breathe life into another human being and or leave the world a little better than it was before we started our day.

They are simple things we can do throughout the day to make a difference. The outcome has nothing to do with and is not dependent upon the realities of our work or home life. They are purposely chosen actions or behaviours that can inspire, encourage, or give hope to another human being or a community and can also make us feel good about our participation by the end of the day.

For example, one of your WRM intentions for the day could be to practice random acts of kindness with every single person you come into contact with (even if they are not kind to you). Other WRM intentions could be to pray for someone who is struggling or make a promise to yourself to eat better so that you feel better and have more to offer to others and yourself. Okay, so if you're reading this and thinking, "That's a nice thought in theory, lady, but the reality of my day does not allow room for yet another 'to do' item on my never ending 'to do' list." If that's your truth, please know that I understand and I hear you!

However, let's do a reality check—those long "to do" lists will probably continue to get longer, and the realities of the workplace and our home life will always be there. So here's some good news: WRM intentions are also a form of self-care. WRM intentions give us a positive daily purpose and allow us to devote a small portion of our day in a controlled, stress-free way. Remember WRM intentions are like eating healthy food, which nourishes us physically, except these daily intentions nourish us emotionally, mentally, *and* physically. They will refuel us!

So here's how to start: Arise, give thanks, and state your WRM intentions (remember, don't get out of bed until you've made that commitment to yourself). Once you've stated your WRM intentions, you should ask yourself four important questions. First, are the WRM intentions realistic? Can I make this happen in the midst of my busyness today? Second, do they align with my value system? Third, will my intentions have a lasting impact? In other words, will bringing my intentions to fruition breathe life and hope into another human being? And finally, can that hope and life have a rippling impact on an even larger community? So, for example, if I am kind to the stranger I meet, it increases the likelihood that the stranger will in turn pass that kindness on to someone else. The *paying-it-forward* concept!

One of the areas I intentionally focus in on each day is staying connected to a force that is bigger than I am.

That force is God. I focus on God because I do not have the intellectual, spiritual, emotional, or physical capacity to handle the issues of today's world by myself. I also focus on how I interact with people through the words that I use, the tone of my voice, and my body language. How I treat a person will impact how they treat the next person they come into contact with.

At the end of the day, it doesn't matter what I have been doing or how much I have accomplished or earned if I haven't treated myself and other people well. If I haven't touched another heart and soul, none of it really matters. I see the WRM intentions as the foundational element I need to keep me grounded in the midst of all of life's busyness. It is a piece of my day that I can take total control of and be proud of. WRM intentions give us meaning in a world that sometimes appears so meaningless.

I find that following through on my stated intentions each day allows me to be in a space where I not only control the outcome but I feel motivated and inspired because of the impact. For me, regardless of all the busyness of my day, it's all about the signature—what am I leaving on the hearts and souls of other folks as I go about my busy life?

Here's some more food for thought as you prepare your WRM intention(s) each day:

- ✳ What will those whom I have come into contact with today remember about me?

- ✳ What will they say once I've left the room?

- ✳ How will they feel in my presence?

- ✳ Will they witness God's presence in my actions?

Good, bad, or indifferent, people will always feel our impact. They will always walk away having experienced something. I truly believe that in every movement we make, conversation we engage in, or situation we find ourselves in, our actions and the choices we make we leave our signature on the heart and soul of another human being. Something we said or did will have moved them in a way that they will never forget. Our words and actions can have the opposite effect and break another human being's spirit. We must remember to always elevate each other to a higher level.

I had the distinct pleasure of attending a function one evening for a nurse's week celebration. I was seated next to a gentleman who was one of the top administrators. As we broke bread together and chatted throughout the evening and shared stories about work, family life, and hobbies, I felt this great connection to a man who was so sincere, kind, and bright. I really enjoyed sitting with him. At the end of the evening as we were about to depart ways, he shook my hand and said, "Thank you, Rosita, it was a pleasure meeting you, and I am a better man for having spent time with you this evening." *Wow*, I had no idea! That moment reminded me how important our words are as well as how we treat our fellow brothers and sisters.

When we read the newspaper or listen to the news on TV and see the destruction in many communities across the world and in our own backyard; when we bear witness to human suffering and losses through war, crime, and hate across the world, it can fill us with a sense of *hopelessness*. We often will ask ourselves how we can make a difference in a world that can sometimes appear so cruel and unjust. And how is it that I can have an impact on problems of such magnitude?

My answer? Take the first step, no matter how small or how big—just take the step.

Start right in your own backyard by following through on your WRM intentions each day. Bring a starving heart and soul to life. Spread love and light wherever you go. As recording artist sensation Dionne Warwick sang years ago (and which will hold true for years to come):

"What the world needs now is love, sweet love,
It's the only thing that there's just too little of.
What the world needs now is love, sweet love,
No not just for some but for everyone."

So if love is the answer (and God is love), how can you be the vehicle each day for ensuring that his love is available to everyone you come into contact with? Love is a great healing force, and our nation needs healing. Our busy lives and overflowing calendars cannot be excuses for not doing our part. No, you may not have the power to end the many wars and suffering occurring around the globe right now, even while you are reading these words, but you do have the power to provide hope to those around you who are suffering from the emotional battles and wars that are raging within. Each of us can do our small part in changing the landscape of this huge world. Carefully consider your WRM intentions that you speak out to the universe tomorrow, and make sure by the end of the day you know with your deepest convictions that you have made a difference. *You've Got the Power!*

The Power of a Well-Lived Life!

> "Moment by moment we provide a sneak preview
> of how our life story will end." —Rosita

I am sure you've heard the old adage that boxers don't become champions in the ring. They become champions outside the ring. They are given recognition in the ring, but it's their daily routines that make them champions. It's the constant practice, mentoring, training (mental, physical), proper meals, sleep, reviewing of old fights, and so on that make the difference. Yes, a boxer, like other athletes, will review past performances and learn from the mistakes and determine areas that need improvement.

If you want to have a great life and accomplish goals, you too have to be a champion in your lifestyle, thoughts, and behaviours around the clock. It's a 24/7 commitment. And we all have to constantly review the tapes of our past performances so that we too don't repeat that which did not bring us effective results and so that we can consider ways of improving. Champions also know the taste of defeat, but they always prepare themselves twice as hard for the comeback...if they so choose. Life will also hand you some defeats, some setbacks, but true champions still rise. I was given a great T-shirt with the statement, "Still standing, stronger, better, wiser." I just love it because it reminds me of the true spirit each of us must apply every second of the day.

What are you doing outside of the "ring" each day? How are you preparing yourself for success both on and off the job? Are you thinking like a champion or merely going through the motions and hoping for a positive outcome? Workplace champions start their preparation for work the evening before by establishing bedtime routines that will ensure a good night's sleep. In the morning they do not get out of bed without first giving thanks, stating their intentions, and choosing to prepare themselves for the recognition they hope to receive once they get into the ring.

Do you choose to prepare yourself throughout your day so that at the end of the day you can go home, stare at the man or woman in the mirror, and get the recognition you deserve? Will you see a champion staring back at you in the mirror? Did your daily routine prepare you for that moment? Life truly is about the choices we make.

A mental exercise I do to remind myself how important it is to make a good choice is to visualize a puzzle in a box. Those pieces in the box are my life story. Every day a new piece is added to the box—based on my experiences, the impact I have had on others, and so on. The picture on the outside of that box is created by me, which means I am responsible for what those pieces inside that box look like.

Each of us is the artist of our lives, and we get to paint a bit of the picture of our lives every day. This continues until the day we die. There will always be another piece to add because each day we have life experiences. But one day the puzzle will be completed.

What will it look like? This picture will be your legacy. Each of us has a responsibility to leave our legacy or our significant mark on the world in which we live.

I know of a wonderful soul who each day painted a beautiful picture of life (her daily routines were that of a true champion). I had the privilege and pleasure of seeing what the picture on the outside of her box looked like and was able to witness that final piece being placed in the puzzle. Her name was Jane. She was an educator, and she left her mark wherever she went. I was lucky enough to call her a friend and a mentor. A few years ago at the ripe old age of eighty-six she died. It broke my heart. I learned from her daughter that on her death bed she had her family gather around and they opened a bottle of champagne, at Jane's request, and they celebrated her final moments. Her daughter described how champagne was poured into all the glasses, including her mom's. She said, "We placed a straw in Mom's glass. Mom insisted on making the first toast, and with everything in her she said a few words, and then she took one sip of that champagne, and she died." Her daughter said to me, "Rosita, only you will know what all that meant." And I did. Taking that sip of champagne from that glass for the very last time was just the big exclamation mark indicating that she finished and she finished well.

Jane lived an honourable life; she left her signature on the hearts and souls of everyone she came into contact with in a powerful way. She had a giving, caring, and loving heart. Jane gave unconditionally to her students, colleagues, strangers, friends, community, and to her family. Jane gave until she had absolutely nothing left to give. She came into this world full of giftedness, and she left it empty because she gave away the gifts she been given at birth. And this, folks, is what life is all about. Jane has left a legacy, and a legacy is something that begins with you and is passed on for generations.

Jane has reminded me, and I hope you too, to live each day boldly, leaving no rocks unturned. Stay in touch with the person in the mirror, and be aware of the pieces you are putting in the box each day because the world will continue viewing (or not) your final picture long after you are gone. I believe the final piece of the puzzle that went into Jane's box was her need to celebrate life even as it was ending simply because she had lived!

Fast forward four years later and I am thinking about Jane's memorial—I realize at this moment that the memorial was in recognition of all the great work performed outside of the ring; the life she lived on a daily basis made her a true champion to all of us who attended her final event. She will be my champion forever!

The Power to Dance and Sing!

"There is a songbird in my heart, and she sings unconditionally every day. Her music stirs my soul." —Rosita

"If music be the food of life, play on." —Shakespeare

I have two amazing sons, Joshua (twenty) and Christian (seventeen), and I have watched them look on in surprise, over and over again, when they hear me singing, dancing, and listening to the same music that they do. Christian chuckles when he sees me dancing and has suggested on more than one occasion that my moves are a little outdated. But still I dance and sing. Why? *Simply because it feels so good!* For me it is a form of celebration. When I hear a beat, it's as if my heart sends a message to every cell in my body to start dancing, and I do just that. The music takes me to another world of sheer ecstasy, and I will continue to feast on the beats of the music and shake my hips until there are no more dances left in me.

One of my favourite songs is "I Will Dance Like David." I have also been told by my two sons that my voice is not half bad if I would just bring it down a notch. Yes, I could do that, but half the fun for me is being able to belt out a song as loudly as I like in a way that keeps my heart happy. How beautiful it would be if the whole world released their inhibitions and sang from the depths of their heart and soul and danced just a little more often. In my humble opinion, I think the world would be a better place.

One of the most common phrases in regards to music, used by musicians and non-musicians alike, is "Music is the universal language." I believe this to be true. According to an article I recently read by Sapan Shaw, there are three reasons why music is called the universal language of the world. First and the foremost, music is made up of seven main notes. No matter what part of the world you are in and what instrument you play, all the music created is from these seven notes. There may be different names for all seven notes in different parts of the world, but for the performer, they are still the same. Second, music is a form of art that can reach the deepest parts of your heart and soul. Third, music, like any other language, can elicit any and every type of emotion.

I believe that God has placed a song in all of our hearts, and it is one of the many common threads that can connect not only individuals but nations. Therefore, I think it is our responsibility to sing. Music serves as a built-in healing system that we can access at any given time. It has the power to heal the mind, body, and soul. It has the power to heal the world! I am always amazed at how music can bring nations together during times of devastation and disasters. I think we all remember the power of the songs and videos "We Are the World" and "Tears Are Not Enough" and more recently "Waving Flag," for Haiti. Those songs moved people to action in terms of donating money and in many cases encouraged people to donate their time and to send love and prayers to hurting people. Wow, the power of seven magical notes....

Music is also a great form of self-care, especially on those days when life gets extremely busy and difficult. I travel a lot in my work, so I try to find ways to practice the art of self-care in my travels. Music works for me as I can engage in therapeutic process while driving in the car, waiting at the airport, or even in flight. You will always see me with my iPod and a pair of earplugs. I was raised on music and dance, and it was a constant emotional, mental, physical, and spiritual staple that could be found in my household on any given day. It was a form of self-care that continuously healed and energized us all. My mom loved to sing, my dad tried to sing (smiles), and my sister Shirley could actually sing! In fact, back in the day, she made several hit records. I always remember soulful music coming from any given room in my house, and at any time of the day, I guess you can say, "I've got the music in me!"

Just as the biblical figure David played his lyre to calm troubled King Saul, sweet sounds often refresh the senses, touch the heart, and heal the wounds during difficult times. Saul's experience is echoed in our daily lives. How often have we heard a mother comforting her newborn child with a soft lullaby? Visit any church on a Sunday morning, and you will see how music is used to bring people closer to their God after a stressful week. Shopping outlets and grocery stores have also recognized the power of music on our emotions. It has been determined that the type of music playing will determine how much a customer purchases.

Music can elicit so many different emotions. Music can compel us to laugh, to cry, to worship God. It can calm us or whip us into an emotional, foot-stomping frenzy. Playing "our song" can trigger memories and nostalgic moods. Today programmed music is used to make jogging, walking, and other exercises easier and more fun. In a recent newspaper interview with a top high school runner, the athlete attributed his running success partly to music. According to the article, the runner tunes out distractions and gets the correct mindset by picking the right mood music and running with it. I am sure those of us who like to exercise to music can relate to this factor. At any sporting event that I ever attended, music was used to get the crowd revved up and excited! Music as a healing therapy took off during World War II. Doctors noticed that wounded and shell-shocked soldiers had better rehabilitation rates when they were exposed to music.

So it is without doubt that music has the power to transform and empower. The next time you are having one of those challenging days at work or in general, soothe your heart, soul, and physical well being with your favourite music—bathe in the beauty of its therapeutic value and let every bone in your body experience the sheer joy found in those seven powerful notes. Get out of your chair and wiggle it just a little bit, too!

The Power to Be Happy!

"I refuse to let people steal my happiness. I feel it is my human right to bathe in this joyful exhilaration daily." —Rosita

Remember the 1988 song recorded by Bobby McFerrin, "Don't Worry, Be Happy." I wonder if Bobby McFerrin knows that he wrote my personal anthem when he created this song. Every time I hear it, I smile BIG—because it's a fun song and yet it holds a lot of truth. The song won McFerrin three Grammys for song of the year, record of the year, and best male pop vocal performance. The original video to this song was posted on YouTube three years ago and has had more than fourteen million views. It has a fun little jingle and picks up your spirit, and if you sing it enough times, you really do stop worrying and begin to have a little fun.

It really is sage advice because worry eats away at our happiness, causing feelings of anxiety, fear, and apprehension. In fact, Michael Fordyce, a leading academic in the field, suggests that the most direct way for most people to increase their happiness is to simply stop worrying! Personally, I learned years ago that worrying doesn't make a situation go away, but real or imagined action does. The action can simply be to pray about it and then release it to God, talk about it with a friend, or seek some sound advice on how to let it go. No one needs to hold on to negative energy and worry. So keep Bobby's song in your heart—if you sing it enough times you will be able to convince your mind to not worry. What we think about actually does come to fruition. Here is an excerpt:

> Here's a little song I wrote
> You might want to sing it note for note
> Don't worry, be happy
> In every life we have some trouble
> When you worry you make it double
> Don't worry, be happy

That verse alone has such positive messaging, but not everyone likes positive messaging. I have been called "Pollyanna" one too many times, and frankly it is getting a little old. So here is my message to all those who think I have been taking a few sniffs of Pollyanna cocaine and am completely out of touch with reality, I am not oblivious to the happenings of the world. I do my part to make it a better world. However, life is supposed to be joyful. Yes, I am drug and alcohol free and definitely in touch with reality. I am in your world but not of the world. Each day I choose to make it a good one. When I am blessed with the gift of each breath (and yes, I stay focused on and am aware of each breath I take), it is more than enough to get me energized and excited about the day, regardless of how it unfolds. This mere decision alone to simply choose my mood can have a huge impact on how it does unfold in actuality.

So my formula for happiness is simple: ***choose the mood, count each breath,*** and ***be thankful*** for the 100,800 times your heart beats in a day. Just that simple formula reminds me to live fully each day and embrace the truly astounding miracle of life. Yes, you are a walking miracle. I am fifty-two years of age and to date have had no major health concerns, and I am thankful for that. I don't consider this luck but rather preparedness. I know the value of a good belly laugh, the power of positive thinking, and the importance of surrounding myself with good people, and how those relationships will impact my emotional, mental, physical, and spiritual health and well being. But most importantly I know the value of my relationship with God. His love for me provides me with such incredible joy!

I am asked almost on a regular basis, "Don't you ever have a bad day or feel the impact of stress or experience sad times?" Here's my response: am I sad when my family experiences any kind of pain or sickness? Yes. Am I sad when I lose a family member or close friend to death's call? Absolutely! I call that *the big stuff!* But the minor infractions throughout the day, a mistake on my part, rude people, a contract I didn't land, long line ups, deadlines to meet etc., *nope!* I don't allow the small stuff to mess up my day. I always go back to my formula and choose the mood, count each breath and remain thankful for the 100,800 times my heart beats in a day. This keeps me focused on what really matters in the greater scheme of things. I would suggest that you create a list called "Big Stuff" and place it in your office and in your home in a place that you visit frequently so that it is always staring you in the face, and when the stressors of life invade your space refer to your list. If it's not big stuff, apply the formula and congratulate yourself for taking good care of your health. If it is indeed big stuff, continue to apply the formula but also seek out support systems to help you through the big stuff, including strengthening your faith!

Change, Challenges and Choices— You've Got the Power!

"Anything that is not changing is dying, and that includes you." —Rosita

It has been my privilege and pleasure to work with thousands of individuals dealing with the impact of changes and challenges in the workplace over the past ten years. What an enlightening and engaging experience. I have been in awe with the impact that the handling of change can have on an individual's emotional, physical, spiritual, and mental health if the right resources, support, and information are not provided. I offer easy-to-implement, simple solutions. My approach is three-fold.

First, I ensure that participants understand the importance of connecting to the power they have to produce positive results, even in the midst of change. If participants can connect to this power that each of us has, then they will not feel as fearful, frustrated, and intimidated by the unknown. That power is our authentic truth. The old adage "The truth will set you free" holds a lot of weight. Living in disguise or being untruthful to the core of who you are can throw you off kilter because it is impossible to access your God-given talents, gifts, or skills (which empower us) if you are living a lie about who you really are. One of the greatest capacities we have as human beings is the capacity to fool ourselves.

Authenticity is the foundation that we need to hold us upright emotionally, mentally, physically, and spiritually in the midst of challenging times. Our authentic truth is the keeper of our values, intellectual capacity, belief systems, skills, knowledge, priorities, and wisdom. We all need to find and connect with that space and use it as our pillar of strength. For example, I have met many individuals in the work-place who feel a lot of uncertainty and insecurity when they are called upon to work differently, learn new ways of doing things, or to even think differently. My sense is that they don't believe that they have the ability to cope with uncertainty or to change the way they've always done things, or that they have the skills or mindset to learn new things. It is my job to help individuals understand that they do have the capacity and skills to cope with the challenges and changes in their lives, both on and off the job, and that they also have the ability to learn new things. However they must first understand who they are at the core and be prepared to embrace an ongoing journey of self-awareness.

It is important to understand how you are feeling during any change process and how you are responding, and here's why. Change will put you into a state of transition. Transition is the psychological transformation that everyone goes through in response to any type of change. It is a normal process. I call it the shaking process or the emotional side of change. (Change has two sides: the rational side, which is the actual change being implemented, and the emotional side, as noted above.)

When my son Josh was about nine years old, he received a piggy bank filled with coins for his birthday from one of his friends. I remember seeing him trying to get money out of that bank. It didn't have one of those little pieces at the bottom that you just pull out and the money would fall. No, this child had to work for that money. I remember watching him shaking the piggy bank and one by one (it was a slow process), coins would fall out. However, he had to keep shaking it until he shook enough out to buy what he wanted. So he had to shake the bank until something of value came out. Watching this, I realized that this is similar to what happens to all of us when we experience transition (the psychological transformation)—we will experience this shaking process. However something of value always comes out if we are patient enough and wise enough to recognize it.

Second, I teach the importance of self-care, simply because our health is our wealth. When change happens at such a quick pace, the first thing most people sacrifice is their health. When deadlines are fast approaching and manpower is limited, we skip lunch and the gym, work late hours, and spend sleepless nights wondering if we've done a good enough job and whether or not we will even have a job the next day. As a result, we are tired, stressed to the max, and our health is impacted in unhealthy ways. I encourage participants to focus on realistic and simple ways of taking better care of themselves. Below are the nine self-care tips I offer to folks experiencing change both on and off the job.

1. As noted earlier: ***Embrace your authentic truth.***

2. ***Get a G.R.I.P.***
(Greatness, Resolve, Inspiration, Possibilities)
Greatness: each day when you arise, step into your greatness. You have a vast array of talents abilities and gifts—utilize them to the fullest. You have the ability to do and be things that you cannot even imagine. Believe it and achieve it. ***Resolve*** that you must let go of those things that you cannot control in order to invite new and creative ideas and thoughts. ***Inspiration***: be inspired by the internal flame that burns inside of you. Find your own inner joy and strength. No one else can give that to you. ***Possibilities***—they are endless and can only be taken advantage of if you recognize them and seize the opportunities.

3. ***Turn on your heart power.*** Stay connected to your colleagues on an authentic level. Build great relationships so that you have resources in place to encourage and support you personally and professionally during challenging times. It is easy to pull away from people when times get tough. The nature of our technologically driven society sometimes makes this easy to do; this is why there is so much stress in both our professional and personal lives. As individuals we need the opportunity to share, discuss our feelings, and exchange coping strategies. We need to be in deeply rooted inspiring relationships that will encourage us and remind us that we have what it takes to make it through the change processes. Also remember, change is an opportunity for growth. Sometimes those we least expect to give us support will avail themselves to us if we simply ask. Remember, no one is perfect, including you. Don't limit your relationships to people who walk

like you, talk like you, think like you, or vote like you. Our greatest growth will often come when we step outside the box and start mingling and getting along with folks we may think we have nothing in common with or feel we just cannot get along with.

4. *Detox the box.* Remember those big calendars that we use to post on our refrigerators or on our desks that had the little boxes and we would fill in our appointments and activities for the day. Sometimes we'd even highlight those items that were of priority on any particular day. I don't think they are in much use today with all the technology available. But up until a year ago I still had one dangling from my office wall. I liked it for many reasons—the most important reason was that it reminded me of how one little box could hold so much truth about our daily activities. I would stare at one box on any given day and think *Wow—if I died today, that box and all the others I had completed for the month would define who I was*. It was kind of a snapshot of who I was. It kind of scared me. Those appointments in each of those boxes told my story. I remember staring at that calendar one day and, in particular, those thirty-one boxes for that month, and I realized that those boxes were filled with a lot of stuff but really didn't contain a lot of time for my unwavering faith, my husband and sons, or myself for that matter. It was just filled with all the stuff I had to do for others. Not much mention of the people and things that really filled my heart and soul with joy, nor did it contain allocated time for personal self-care. Everything else took precedence. I realized I had to change this. I had it all wrong. As do most of us. At that point I promised myself that every day for the rest of my life I would

ensure that five important priorities were highlighted in my calendar each day. Namely, faith, my husband Norm, my two sons Josh and Chris, and time for myself (self-care). Anytime I could not make my faith, my family, and my health a priority, I would have to detox by taking something out of the box on that particular day so that I could make time for the things in life that really mattered and that breathed life into my heart, soul, and physical well being. Although sometimes I still don't get it right, I work hard at getting it right the majority of the time.

5. ***Plug your energy leaks.*** Have you experienced a morning when you wake up fired up and ready to take on the world but by about ten o'clock you suddenly feel your energy level starting to slip away? Well you are not alone. The workplace is rampant with energy vampires (i.e., the Debbie Downers), who can knowingly and unknowingly zap your energy. They are the visibly unhappy group of employees who see themselves as victims due to changes and upheavals in the workplace, and they want everyone to know it. Unhappy employees who place themselves in the victim mode only want to be around other disgruntled and unhappy employees. Remember—misery loves company, and only the kind of company that thinks and acts the way they do. So when Bubbly Barbara walks in first thing Monday morning full of life and zest and simply says, "Good morning," Debbie Downer and the Downettes will not be impressed and on many occasions will not even respond. Their body language and demeanour screams "I'm miserable, and you should be too." Ignoring these types of people is not always an option, especially when they sit in the

cubicle next to you. So what is Bubbly Barbara to do when by ten o'clock the bubbles have started to fizzle and she slowly feels her energy being sucked out of her? Remember what we spoke about in previous chapter: *choose the mood, count each breath, and be thankful* for the 100,800 times your heart beats in a day. Adopt your "Don't worry, be happy" motto and keep your intentions close to your heart. Finally, simply demonstrate (through your actions, responses, and behaviour) your more positive approach to dealing with change, and hopefully it will rub off. Don't under any circumstances invest time in trying to change that person; feel the love and focus on your health and be the change you would like to see.

6. *Give something away.* Every day we should make it a habit to give something away that will add joy to another person's day. It does not have to be expensive or time consuming in order to make it happen. Keep it simple, and feel the impact on both you and the other person. For example, give away a genuine compliment or a smile. You never know the impact. For example, I had a friend who had cancer, and she said every day while all her other friends were at work she would go down to the waterfront, sit on a bench, and be inspired by all the smiles she collected. She said each of those smiles provided her with great healing. It gave her energy and a real sense of hope. It made her realize how important people are in our lives, even strangers just passing by. I wonder if they knew the joy they brought to my dear friend.

7. *Zip it and flip it—for the health of it!* I have learned in life that you do not have to respond to

every comment that is made about you (especially if it is offensive to you) or a situation you may be in. My husband has mastered that art, but I am still working on it. Like most others, I have this great need to respond. The need to set the other person straight. To get back at them. That is just our ego and flesh responding in a way that is not nurturing to our emotions. Sometimes the best response is no response!

8. *Laugh until it hurts.* The shortest distance between two people is laughter. Turn some of those challenges into chuckles. Sometimes we just need to deal with stress with a chuckle or two. It is great for your health. Two minutes of anger can impact your immune system in a negative way for up to five hours. One minute of laughter can boost your immune system for up to twenty-four hours. What a great healing tool laughter can be!

9. *Don't drop the glass balls.* I teach a lot about work/life balance. It's a hot topic right now in the workplace. All the demands of changes and challenges and our responses to the changes are leaving us feeling like the monkey in the middle with the stressors of work and home vying for our attention. We often find ourselves juggling too many balls with the fear of possibly dropping one or all of them. I suggest to my participants that although we may drop a ball or two along the way, there are some balls that we cannot afford to drop at any cost. They are the *glass* balls. I ask participants to pick three things in life that mean more to them than life itself (the glass balls) and to make a decision that those three glass balls will under no circumstance be a part of the juggling act. Once you drop the glass balls, unlike the rubber balls, they don't bounce

back. Instead, they shatter into pieces. For example, my three glass balls are my faith, my family, and my health. Those three things will always be first on my list, and I choose not to sacrifice them, regardless of what is going on in my life. I have made a promise to myself to always honour my glass balls and to ensure that they get first priority in my life, not just some days but every day! Whenever I am giving self-care tips, the glass balls are the tip that resonates the most with my participants. Later on in another chapter, I will share how a participant helped me come up with his amazing self-care tip.

Third, I remind participants that everyone will move through the change process at a different pace, simply because we are all different. Be patient with each other. A lot of the stress associated with change comes from work mates not understanding their peers' response to change and that not everyone travels at the same speed through the process. Be kind to yourself and each other during times of change, ask for help, and tap into any additional resources your workplace may be offering to support you during this time.

The Power of the Mirror

"My opinions of others oftentimes reflect back to me
my opinion of myself." —Rosita

My mama taught me one of the most valuable lessons in life: she always reminded me of the importance of not judging and finding fault in others, but rather to look at myself first and then perhaps I wouldn't be so tough on others. I think what she was in essence telling me was that if I took a really good look at myself, I would soon notice that I too was not perfect and did indeed have many little flaws of my own. I guess it's kind of like that biblical reference from Matthew 7:5, which reads "You hypocrite, first take the plank out of your own eye, and then you will see clearly to remove the speck from your brother's eye."

Wise words from my mama, but I have to admit they are not easy to live by. Why? Because God gave me a tongue and I talk too much, and with that much talking I am bound to mess up along the way. I do, however, make a daily effort to live by this model. I get it right about 75 percent of the time; however, there are still those days when my tongue kicks into gear before my brain, and I find myself falling into that old trap again, judging and scrutinizing others unfairly. So I have recently devised a little plan that has assisted me in embracing my mama's philosophy for life. Regardless of the situation that I am in, before I open my mouth I do the following;

1. I ask God to make his presence known, because on my own I am weak and my tongue is a dangerous instrument. Sometimes it's hard to believe the kind of power this small instrument has. It can build people up or tear them down. It can be our strength or our weakness. Words that flow from our lips on an ongoing basis can be very destructive or they can build people up!

2. I look deep into the individual's eyes and am reminded that they are a precious child of God.

3. I ask myself what is it that I can say or do that would make that person's day better than it already is, regardless whether it is a good encounter or not. After all, anyone can be pleasant when the exchange is good, but what if someone is simply not being nice to you? My advice is to smother them with kindness. Please note, however, that if you are being abused or bullied, that is considered assault and not the type of interactions I am referring to here.

I have also learned from my Mama that my opinion of someone, especially if it is not nice, is more of a reflection of me more than it is of the other person. So if it's nice, that reflects nicely on me and says a lot about me as a person. If it is not nice, then again it speaks volumes about me. So the bottom line is that whatever comes out of our mouths is a reflection of who we are. That wisdom taught to me by my mama at an early age has kept me on a journey that is laced with self-awareness, emotional intelligence, humility, and respect for everyone, even if I don't think they deserve it, because it is not my job to judge. I will leave that to God.

The Power to Smile B.I.G.—
Be an Inspiration for God

"The best time to smile is when you really don't feel like it."
—Rosita

I am standing in line at a grocery store and am mesmerized by the faces that pass me by. I can't find a smile or a grin on any one of them even though I make an attempt to smile nicely at a few people in close proximity. Everyone is in a hurry, distracted, pressured by timelines and overbooked schedules. At least that's how it appears. A few folks look at me as if to say "What's your problem, lady, I don't know you!" For the remainder of the day, I am determined that I can collect some smiles from the folks who pass me by. I collect a few, but hardly any in comparison to the number of people I came into contact with.

C'mon people, a smile costs absolutely nothing and it can warm the heart and soul of another human being, not to mention the benefits it can bring to the one giving the smile. The ability to smile is a gift, although probably one of the most underrated of all the gifts we have. We have an incredible tool at our disposal. Research has proven that when you turn that frown upside down, there is a shift in energy and mood-enhancing hormones are released. Mother Teresa put is so nicely when she was quoted as saying, "I will never understand all the good that a simple smile can accomplish"

So where have all the smiles and joyful bliss of everyday living gone? I guess the fancy cars and over-sized house didn't do it for us? Were they supposed to? It seems as though our busy schedules both at home and on the job have some of us in a tizzy, coupled with the everyday realities of life. Stress has become a lifestyle. As I was driving home from a day of attempting to collect smiles, a thought came to mind: *Perhaps I am being too judgmental.* I'd better go back to my mama's wisdom: I really don't know what is going on in the lives of these strangers. How huge were the burdens they were carrying? I have no real way of knowing. Could my smile have made a difference? I believe so. On my drive home, a couple of thoughts ran through my head: *Have we as a society lost touch of the reality of life and living? Are we searching for a utopian lifestyle?* Is this what we are hoping to find at the end as we make our way through the daily stressors of life and work? Will that bring the smiles back?

Perhaps I will give a quick reality check here. There will be pain, joy, sickness, health issues, babies will be born, some will die, cancer will strike some someone close to you, unemployment rate is at an all time high, many of us are at risk for diabetes, heart disease and a number of immune system deficiencies because of the choices we make, the divorce rate is at a all time high, and the list goes on and on. We can control some of these things, and other things, well, they're just life!

Okay, so you are probably thinking, if this is the reality of living, what's there to smile about, right? I think if you are reading this page right now you have everything to smile about because you have eyesight, you are alive, and your brain is active. How beautiful is that? Still not convinced? Go look at your local newspaper and read the obituaries. I bet your name is not there! How awesome is that? If I were you I'd smile big! Life will not always hand us a bowl of cherries, but if we focus on the *big stuff,* which is really the fact that we are breathing at this moment, then regardless of all the other little things that life will deal us each day, we will remember to smile as a form of thanksgiving and appreciation.

I have lost love ones to death's calling, have dealt with suicide of a close family member, have caused others pain (I'm no saint), and others have caused me pain, but here's the good news: I have something available to me that is so powerful and can get me through every second of the day, and it's my God-given freedom to choose! Each of us is always one choice away from the type of day we'd like to have or the type of life or dream we'd like to bring to fruition. Yet many of us walk around as though all choices have been taken away from us. *News flash,* they haven't.

Choose to smile every day; it will increase your energy level and lift your emotional or mental state. As a result, you will have a more productive day. Smiles are also contagious! You give a smile away and you feel great, and the person receiving it feels so wonderful that they in turn pass it on.

It's a great way to change the world for the better—join the movement—one smile at a time.

The Power of Self-Motivation

"Motivation is an inside job." –Rosita

It is no secret that I have found my passion for life. I have unwrapped the gift that God has placed inside of me, and as a result it has granted me an abundance of opportunities, has awakened my inner being with delight, and continually allows me to have a positive impact on everyone I come into contact with. Lack of motivation has never been an issue for me because it is my firm belief that once you connect to your passion or purpose, you become so intoxicated with a feeling of joy that even the thought of using your giftedness sets you on fire!

Self-motivation, I believe, is fuelled by purpose and passion and your ability to be in alignment with your authentic truth. Self-motivation allows us to realize our goals, dreams, and aspirations. It is the tool we require to move forward and leave our mark on the world. It is driven by our own personal desires and not those that someone else has laid out for us.

Ask any successful person the key to their success, and they will always tell you that they found their purpose and passion in life and therefore they are motivated to bring their passion to life. It is difficult to succeed without self-motivation. We all need a *motive* to spark a flame of action.

I get concerned when people call me and say, "I am looking for a motivational speaker," because the inference is that I have the power to motivate a group of people, and I don't. I eloquently tell people that I am a speaker who happens to be motivated and that I can support people on their journey to finding self-motivation but that I don't have the power to motivate people. The fact that I am self-motivated may inspire people to action, but they must have the motive, purpose, or drive to make whatever it is they are trying to do happen. I believe that each of us has the powerful tool of motivation within us. It is up to each of us individually to ignite it so that we can use our talents, skills, knowledge, and creativity to produce positive results. Furthermore, we need to tap into this powerhouse in order to create ongoing abundance, good health, good choices, great relationships, and achievements. Much of what we desire in life can happen if self-motivation is there! Self-motivation is often hidden beneath exhaustion, frustration, disappointments, negative thoughts, etc., but it is indeed there.

Do you want to be on fire? Do you want to be your absolute best both on and off the job every day? Do you want to live life with passion and on purpose? Well here are seven must do's if you want to make it happen:

1. Understand that self-motivation is inspired by purpose, a deep-rooted passion that is connected to your giftedness. It is the *why* factor. Understanding your purpose or *why* factor will inspire and motivate you because it will unleash your giftedness. Simply put, "why" were you created? Utilizing your gift to the

fullest is what brings you joy and inspiration each day; it motivates you because you are doing what you love and comes naturally to you.

Fact Check: People with self-motivation have a purpose. Their passion is their work, not the by-product of their work. Of course, they appreciate the by-product, but they love their work more. Happy and self-motivated employees go the extra mile; they are significantly more productive, efficient, and reliable than those employees who are not self-motivated. Don't get stuck at "how" to make this happen; if you have a strong enough *why,* you will overcome any *how.* Be patient, be still, and be open to possibilities.

2. Motivation is internal. External motivation is just a temporary fix. As I mentioned earlier, I can't bring motivation to anyone, nor can others; it must come from within. When the *why* factor kicks in, you will be honouring your calling and self-motivation will ooze out of every fibre of your body.

Fact check: It is estimated that only 5 percent of the population in the world are self-motivated or they consciously choose what to be motivated about. *They disregard their current situation, their inner voices, and all external factors and or distractions.* This group takes charge over their lives, and they utilize the power within to accomplish their heart's desire. The other 95 percent are motivated by something else. The factors include other people, current feelings and circumstances, doubtful inner voices, or accidental means. This group reacts to their life circumstances and often sees themselves as victims of circumstance. They spend a lot of time and money searching for motivation in various external sources (temporary fixes) for their shot of energy and motivation, and when they come off their high they go back to their source for more motivation. Imagine that 95 percent of the world falls into this category; it is no surprise that the self-help industry is a multi-billion-dollar industry. The way out of this dilemma is to learn how to be self-motivated.

3. Listen to your thoughts. Self-talk is influential—talk success and good things into your life.

Fact check: Self-talk is the voice of your thoughts, the incessant inner dialogue within your head. It is ever changing according to your experience, feelings, and moods—like a magnet, your inner dialogue attracts a reflection of itself. Thus negative, toxic talk attracts negative toxic outcomes and attitudes and becomes the root cause of our experience.

4. Boost your energy level regularly through self-care; coffee is only a temporary fix.

Fact check: Exercising and sleeping well help too. You should also watch out for sugary foods. The "sugar blues" kill motivation. Once you find energy boosters that work for you, make a list and keep it handy for future use. Also, watch what you're listening to, who you are hanging out with, and what you are watching on TV.

5. Call back motivational feelings. Remember and experience what it felt like at a time when you did feel self-motivated. This is a benchmark that will remind you how it feels to be motivated. This is that great feeling or your *anchor!* Capture that exhilarating moment, clench your fist tight, and *anchor it*. Create a next moment from that place.

6. Move towards things that are compelling and away from those things that are not.

7. Applaud and celebrate your daily successes.

Nothing is going to happen in any area of your life until you choose to do something. However powerful the engine of your car is, it isn't going anywhere until you take it out of the garage and out on the highway. Dig deep down within yourself and let your engine stir up self-motivation—the journey will be never ending.

The Power of the Pieces

"What if my life was played out on a big movie screen?
Would it be 'Oscar' worthy?" —Rosita

Do you remember your excitement as a kid putting your first puzzle together? I certainly remember my children and their excitement as they examined the picture on the box, poured the pieces out on the table, and began building their masterpiece. What excitement when they produced the finished picture. But what frustration if the last piece required to complete the masterpiece was missing. As a mother I could never find peace until I helped them find the missing piece, which was usually tucked beneath something on the table or oftentimes was under the table. I loved the look on their faces when that piece appeared because now they could admire their finished product.

Do you have peace? Is there a missing piece in your present life that is interfering with you having peace? For example, for me, if I do not have God in my life, I cannot experience peace. When I am in conflict with other people, peace cannot find its way into my heart. I have to first find the pieces that are causing me to not have peace and find a way to have them add value to my life. Thinking about this reminds me of the peace that I think we all diligently search for; when we find it, we do everything possible to hang on to it. I believe that finding, holding on to, and enjoying this peace has so much to do with the complete picture of all the pieces in our life at any given time. If someone were to hand you a box with your name on it and tell you that the puzzle represents all that you are and all that you have become up until this moment, would you want to put it together and on display for everyone to see, or would you be frustrated because there were so many missing pieces without any explanation? And no, they are not hidden under an item on the table or underneath the table. Think about the power you have to find the missing pieces, as you go through the day and find yourself frustrated by minor things. Maybe the solution is to find the missing pieces, so you can have peace of mind!

The Power of Friendships!

Thank you for being a friend.
Travel down the road and back again.
Your heart is true; you're a pal and a confidant.
And if you threw a party,
Invited everyone you knew.
You would see the biggest gift would be from me
And the card attached would say,
Thank you for being a friend.
—By Andrew Gold; recorded by Cynthia Fee

Remember that theme song from the popular TV show, Golden Girls? I love the message of that short song, and I loved the show. It was such fun tuning in and watching the ups and downs and hilarious journey of four women who had become roommates and friends. There was never a dull moment, kind of like the friendships many of us have. This chapter is dedicated to all the Golden Girls (friends) who have impacted my life. However I would also like to give a shout out to the many other women who have been a part of my journey.

I have five sisters, several sisters-in-law, and a host of beautiful women friends. In my travels as a speaker,

I have had the pleasure of meeting some of the most amazing women on this planet. I belong to one of the largest women's volunteer organizations in the world, Zonta International. There too, I am surrounded by beautiful, phenomenal women, and I am a better person because of it.

It is true that every person or friendship we commit to breathes life into another unique part of our personality. But those special Golden Girls will breathe life into you at an even deeper level. I am a very transparent person, and authenticity is my middle name, but there are a few personality bloopers I have that I would prefer to keep between me and my Golden Girls. This is the coolest thing about having a deep bond with women—it is a special sisterhood, and when you're with your golden girlfriends, they make you feel as though you are the most important person in the world. They know your deepest secrets and your personality quirks and they love you just the way you are. They support you, cheer you on, encourage you and lift you up when you need it most. They breathe life into you during troubled times. I am so glad that God gives us special girlfriends and women folk who fuel our spirits.

As a woman with authentic power and grace and an abundance of women folk and golden girlfriends to support me, I feel truly blessed. During what can sometimes be very stressful times in our lives, both on and off the job, it is that cup of coffee with our girlfriends that helps us find our *mojo* again.

"It is not the friends in your life but the life in your friends."—Anonymous

My life has been truly blessed because of my close friendships and also other fun gals who have impacted my life, perhaps without even knowing it. They are the people who come into your life if only for a short time, and they leave you a better person because of it. I'd like to thank those women folk as well. And to all my new friends that I continuously make each day through my work and volunteer activities, you *rock!*

And to my really close gal pals (the ones whose secrets I hold in my heart and who are the keeper of mine), the following is dedicated to you:

> The soul of a woman is laced with honesty, truth and integrity, grace, confidence, and poise. It has tasted the pain of grief, disappointment, and rejection. Yet her inward fire is ignited by and continuously burns with passion and refuses to go out. It is radiant, powerful, hungry, desirable, and intellectually capable of attracting all that she desires. Her spirit refuses to die. It dances, sings, and celebrates all day and through the wee hours of the night, even when she is fast asleep. Life is all she knows; she refuses to entertain the company of darkness. On rare occasions when darkness dances around her heart and soul, she exposes it with the light of the most high God. She is that songbird that sings when an unexpected curve ball comes her way. She takes her cues from an amazing God. She is never afraid.

I think every woman should surround herself with Golden Girls—I certainly have. Here is my acronym for the Golden Girls in my life:

G—Gregarious
O—Open Minded
L—Loyal
D—Dependable
E—Enthusiastic
N—Nice

Thank you, my gregarious, open-minded, loyal, dependable, enthusiastic, and nice pals. I use the power of our friendships as fuel on those days when I need a little lift!

The Power of Being Awake!

JUST LIVIN' THE DREAM (NOT)

Limitations are an illusion
Stifling ambitions and dreams
We sleep in ignorance
Of our role as creators
Accepting the role of pawns
On life's chess board
Our greatness
Kept secret from the masses
Lest we decide
To throw off the harness
Of helplessness
And embrace
Power
Beyond
Our
Wildest
Imagination
Now
Is the time to
Wake up
–Alison Stormwolf, 2007

I agree whole heartedly with Alison Stormwolf—it is time to *wake up!* Limitations are an illusion and, yes, the mindset of limitations or scarcity mindset leaves us in a sleepy state of ignorance and we become pawns in the game of life, never truly becoming all that we were created to be and created to have. I believe that each of us came into this world fully loaded with authentic grace, truth, wisdom, intellect, giftedness, and our own unique power. However, I think we need to raise the frequency of our mindset and listen to the wisdom of our heart and soul at the deepest level, where spirit resides, and tap into that amazing power and truth about ourselves, all that is available to us.

Instead we allow our egos to take flight and run around in hysterics saying, "I have to do more, I have to be more, I have to compete in order to get my portion, there's not enough, we'd better get tougher." If struggling is the way to get there, we'd all be there by now. Especially in a world where the constant message we hear is "not enough." That very act of struggle keeps us stressed, scared, diseased, and on the edge 24/7. Our competitive nature and scarcity mentality is driving us all just a little closer to heart disease, immune system deficiencies, sleep disorders, psychological disorders, and the list goes on and on. We have to slow down, take a deep breath, and realize that we are all uniquely created and powerful. Now is the time to tap into our uniqueness and use this power given to us by our creator to achieve that which we deserve and to use it in a way that not only empowers us but everyone we come into contact with on a daily basis. It's time to make a shift in our mindset. How do we shift our mindset?

1. Reject our attachment to ego and our old ways of thinking and being in order to break free from the trance of scarcity.
2. Recognize that we have greatness and that God's Holy Spirit is within us.
3. Spend time in the spiritual realm, in quiet meditation; don't let the noise drown out spirit.
4. Use our spiritual GPS to navigate through the busyness of the day.
5. Let go of our clenched fists (which symbolize our need to hold on to everything) and open up both hands to receive the abundance of blessings awaiting us each and every day.

Practicing these five simple steps each day will free our mind and allow us to stand back once in awhile and take an inventory of "stuff" we are holding on to that is in actuality trapping us into an abyss. It will also allow us to connect with what truly matters, awaken our authentic truth, and stay connected to the source that brings true abundance and joy to our lives. It's not about holding on, competing with others, living with a scarcity mentality, and collecting stuff; but rather it is about collecting hearts and building amazing relationships with everyone we come into contact with. *Wake up!* It's time to start truly living.

The Power of the R.O.A.R.

"Yes, I am my sister's keeper, and it is my responsibility to reach down and pull her up when she has fallen." —Rosita

My passion for women's issues started at a very young age. Seeing my amazing mother raise fourteen children to adulthood with such passion, love, and strength made me realize just how absolutely resilient women really are. My mom was resourceful and courageous and made each and every one of us feel special, as if we were her only child. When I look back, I realize the strength and tenacity this took. I knew growing up I wanted to live out those characteristics that my mother portrayed and that I also wanted to encourage other women to do the same. My mother made me believe that anything was possible because I saw her do so much with so little. I witnessed her quiet strength during some insurmountable challenges in her life as a mother and wife. What I admired the most was that she always kept a positive disposition and could always see the light at the end of the tunnel. Yes, I am my mother's daughter. "I am strong, I am invincible, I am woman." Those powerful words are from a song by Helen Reddy, entitled "I Am Woman." These lyrics have been deeply ingrained in my heart and soul from the moment I first heard them back in the '70s. The song was an empowerment anthem for many women, and today is still recognized as such. Reddy was quoted as saying, "The composition was the result of my search for a song that would express my growing passion for female empowerment."

I think it's time for women to start roaring again, and I think the roar has to come from within. I come into contact with so many women in the workplace in my job as a speaker, and many relay to me that they are tired, stressed, trying to find balance, trying to get along with their co-workers, and the list goes on and on. Where has the *roar* gone? Why are we meowing, whining, and complaining? Where has the voice of empowerment gone? You know, the voice that said, "I am strong, I am deserving, and so are all my other sisters in the workplace and around the world." Are we still elevating and encouraging each other? Are we competing with each other or are we completing each other?

It is no secret that the current economic situation coupled with the challenges of change has resulted in stress being at an all-time high. It is because of this that we need to come together and support each other as women and not tear each other down. We need to be patient with each other, reach out to each other, and love each other unconditionally. It is time for us to rise up, to extend a hand both on and off the job, and encourage our stressed-out sisters, instead of judging and gossiping about them. We are women—that's our bond, and we share many of the same stressors. Let us unite and be a source of hope and inspiration for each other. We must constantly be paying attention to how we are shaping our lives because we are the role models for the future generation of women and young girls.

In the workplace, we can start this process by simply being kinder to one another, holding off on judgemental critiques, building internal support systems, developing woman-to-woman mentoring programs or lunch time forums where women can come together, connect, converse, and cheer each other on. We also need opportunities to celebrate our daily successes.

If this happens, we will stop hearing the gossiping and draining meows and start hearing and seeing women R.O.A.R. (Reaching Out And Responding) in a manner that will allow each of us as women to:

✴ Feel good about ourselves and what we do

✴ Respond better to stressful situations

✴ Tap into the resources available, including other women folk

✴ Take better care of ourselves

✴ Capitalize on the many opportunities that await us each day

✴ Feel empowered by our own strength as well as the strength of all our sisters who stand by us because they want to see us win.

This is a fire-proof formula if we want to collectively R.O.A.R. so that our voices are heard and the impact is felt around the world.

The Power to Recognize the Heart of Leadership

"Sometimes the head has to follow the heart." –Rosita

Almost twenty-seven years ago I was offered my first (unsolicited) professionally paid leadership position. I think I was offered this position mainly because I was well liked and had great people skills, a passion for bringing out the best in people, and tons of energy, plus I was gutsy and didn't take no for an answer. Hmmm...Sounds like the right formula for successful leadership, doesn't it? At the time, however, I didn't realize it. Little did I know that twenty-seven years ago I had all the ingredients that so many leadership gurus are now writing and speaking about (and bringing in mega bucks with their value-added plethora of books, CDs and videos). I guess I missed that boat; call me naive.

Vince Lombardi, one of the greatest NFL coaches of all time and an astute businessman, was addressing a large corporate audience. He said, "I am going to share with you the key to success in any business." He said, "The secret, in a word, is *heart power*." Capture the heart, and you've captured the person. In my humble opinion, you will also capture the talents, skills, expertise, and passion of the individual, and they will fall in love with the vision and mission of the company and create unwavering success. However, continuous maintenance work along the way is a requirement. A good leader checks in with their people on a regular basis to ensure that they have the resources they need to complete their assigned tasks and to give feedback and see how the members of the team are doing. Great leaders know that it is imperative to support the emotional, physical, and mental wellness of every staff member.

My leadership position was that of Executive Director of a non-profit organization, a position I held for over twenty years. As I reflect back upon what made it a uniquely run and successful organization, it was indeed heart power that flowed through the organization at every level. It was the fuel that kept the team together and results unfolding. The office was full of highly motivated, energized, and authentically passionate and committed folks. This happened because the leadership team was able to capture hearts.

We built relationships with the staff by eating lunch together, taking coffee breaks together, and showing an interest in each other's lives. We got to know our employees at a soul level. We showed we cared and were interested in their passions both on and off the job. We truly cared about our people. And as a result, they gave us all they had and always exceeded expectations. Although this is much easier to do in a small organization, I certainly do not want to dismiss it as impossible in large organizations. It can happen regardless of the size of the organization; you just have to understand its significance and impact on the bottom line, and then train and encourage your managers/supervisors/team leaders and incorporate this relationship-building piece into a strategic process.

I often hear people say, "Yes, I know relationship building is important, but who has time?" And there is often no follow through and no accountability built into their strategic process. Our greatest need as human beings is relational. We want to be in relationships that will inspire, encourage, educate, and move us to higher levels professionally and personally. Great leaders will set both organizational and personal goals with the top one being to improve or continue building heart connections with those they lead. No one will follow you if you show absolutely no genuine interest in them as a human being. People are the greatest asset, and your organization must demonstrate this by making sure they know just how important they are as individuals first!

It is one thing to have the head knowledge, but that is not what will sustain a business. Sustainability is connected to heart-to-heart relationships. Yes, you can build a business without those connections, I know it has been done, but in most cases it has not been sustained over the long haul. Bottom line, you always want to make people feel needed and as if they are the most important person on the face of the earth. Mary Kay Ash, founder of Mary Kay, Inc., once said that she always made sure that when she was in anyone's presence she imagined that they were wearing a sign around their neck that said, "Make me feel important," and that is exactly what she did. This is a key component of her extremely successful and sustainable business power!

Mary Kay Ash also believed that those relationships we have outside of the workplace also play a critical role in the success of an organization. She once commented, "The real success of our personal lives and careers can best be measured by the relationships we have with the people most dear to us, our family, friends, and co-workers. If we fail in this aspect of our lives, no matter how vast our worldly possessions or how high on the corporate ladder we climb, we will have achieved very little." Imagine working for a woman this emotionally intelligent and caring. She knew how to take care of her employees.

According to leadership guru Mac Anderson, from his book *The Essence of Leadership*, one of the keys to building heart power is establishing trust. How do you establish this trust that Mac is referring to? In my opinion, it is really a simple process based on a deep desire and genuine commitment to really getting to know others at the core. Not just for the sake of producing results but because you have a genuine interest and passion for the human spirit. It is about deeply caring for others, what they are concerned about the most, their dreams and passions, and what brings them to life the most. Building this authentic bond will grow the roots of trust, the foundation to great relationships, and thus sustainable success.

Leadership is about creating a way for people to contribute to making something extraordinary happen. Two more critical leadership principles also need to be incorporated in this time of unprecedented change. First, we need to engage collective leadership throughout our organizations. Collective leadership is a about creating a culture where everyone is encouraged to recognize their expertise and leadership abilities. It is also one in which followers become leaders and leaders know when to follow. People need to be engaged in leadership regardless of whether or not they have the title. Why? Because in the age of change and complexity, an organization's success will depend on its ability to grow and develop its leaders. Of course not everyone in the organization will have the same leadership capacity, skills, or training, but when we bring them all together, the organization becomes unstoppable because you will be using the human potential of the entire collective, not just the chosen few.

Second, for organizations to thrive during this robust time of change there needs to be ongoing leadership development coupled with knowledge of how to respond to change. This too should be a part of the strategic plan, and there should be resources set aside in order to make this a reality. When budgets have to be cut, organizations often decrease or even eliminate their professional development line. This is a mistake because the only way you will grow your organization is by growing your people. Long gone are the days of the leader who walked in and took up all the space in the room. Great leaders walk into a room and create space for other people, a space where people can unleash their talents and generate new and improved ideas.

In summary, the reality of leadership requires six key components: 1. develop heart-to-heart relationships, built on trust and mutual respect; 2. equip your staff with the resources they require to succeed in their day-to-day activities; 3. elevate and release individual potential; 4. promote emotional, mental, and physical wellness; 5. engage in collective leadership; and 6. provide ongoing professional development. This will increase the likelihood that your agency or place of business stays ready to lead through the realities of the twenty-first-century workplace.

The Power to Win Big!

"Oh what a disappointment to get to the end of our lives and realize that we didn't live." –Rosita

Today I hit the *jackpot!* I mentioned this excitement to a woman at the gym. She was so intrigued and excited for me until she asked, "What did you win?" and I responded, "Another day!" She said, "Oh, yea, that's good," but I could tell she was expecting a different response. She was impressed with my positive attitude, but at the same time slightly disappointed. But really, how much better does it get than waking up to see another day? If my calculations are right, since my time here on earth I have hit the jackpot exactly 18,980 times (don't bother doing the math—I am fifty-two years old). How awesome is that? So how many times have you hit the jackpot?

Have you been taking your winnings for granted? I will take winning this daily jackpot over any of the others that require me to pick a number, scratch a ticket, play the slots, or place a bet. None of those could ever guarantee as big a payoff as the one I keep cashing in on each morning when I arise to a new day. So my stakes are on the one that gives life.

Oh, how good it is to be alive. Have you thought about that lately? I heard this wonderful story many years ago about a professor who was explaining to a former student the importance of appreciating the time given to us and not taking a single breath for granted. He spoke about how special Saturdays were in his life. He mentioned that because his weekdays were so full, he always set Saturday aside for him and his wife and absolutely nothing interfered with that time. He said every Saturday morning they would start their day off with breakfast at their favourite restaurant and then spend the rest of the day together. He then spoke about buying some marbles and placing them in a jar, which he kept on his kitchen counter. He said that he understood that the average life expectancy is about seventy-five years. He acknowledged that some live more and some a little less, but on average folks live about seventy-five years. He multiplied seventy-five times fifty-two and came up with 3900, which is the number of Saturdays an average person has in their entire lifetime. He then multiplied his current age by fifty-two and then subtracted that number from 3900 and realized that he had already lived over 2800 Saturdays. It occurred to him that if he lived to be seventy-five he only had about a thousand of them left to enjoy. So he went to every toy store and bought up a thousand marbles and placed them in a clear plastic container. Every Saturday since then he takes one out and throws it away. Watching the marbles diminish helps him focus on the really important things in life. He went on to say, "By the way, last Saturday I took my last marble out, so every Saturday now is a bonus." I love that story. The professor knew the value of a day.

From the first time I heard that story several years ago, it impacted me profoundly. It is one of those stories you never forget. I'm not sure if I could actually place the number of marbles in a jar based on my time left on earth. I might cringe when I get to that last marble, not because it symbolizes the end or the coming to the end (because I have lived a great life) but rather because living is just so much fun!

If you really want to appreciate each day just a little bit more, wake up each morning realizing that you really did win the jackpot. If you really want to understand this at a different level, do as the professor did: calculate your approximate time left on earth and place some a marbles in a container for the number of Saturdays (or whatever day you'd like to pick) you have left. What a great way to have a reality check once a week. I want to hit the jackpot each day for many more days to come. But the professor's wisdom is so on target. We will eventually lose all of our marbles (no pun intended), and when I get to my last marble, I think I shall pray for some bonus rounds because I just love living so much!

I had another one of those jackpot moments a couple of months ago. I was hired to do a presentation to a group of government employees on how to reduce stress. The session was held in a church hall. When I arrived, I had a difficult time finding parking, which I assumed was on the street as I saw no way of getting into a parking lot at the church. After circling the block a few times, I noticed a small laneway on the left-hand side of the church. I drove in only to find a couple of parking spaces that were reserved for the minister and clergy. I was about to back out when I discovered another laneway and at the end of it I could see that several cars were parked. *Aha*, I thought, *this must be the parking area*. Thank goodness, as I was running a little late. As I began driving down this laneway, I noticed a cemetery to both my right and my left. At the end of the lane there was indeed lots of parking. This was obviously where the participants for my session had parked. I got out of my car and started walking back up the laneway towards the church.

As I was walking, I realized just how very close I was to the tombstones on either side of me, so close, in fact, that I could have touched them. I remember smiling as I walked through and thinking *oh how good it is to be alive*! I walked into that session feeling more pumped than I ever thought I could be. Eureka! I had another jackpot experience! As I walked into the room where I would be presenting, everyone in that session looked dead, exhausted, or stressed. *Wow*, I thought, *did they just walk up the same pathway that I did?* After my introduction, I decided to ask the group that very question, and when I did, they all just looked at me as if to say, "What is she talking about?" So I said, "How many of you are a little stressed and could use a little inspiration?" Every hand in the room went up, as expected. I then repeated my original question, "Did you all walk up the same path I did after you parked your cars?" They all nodded their heads (okay, so they are getting it now, or so I thought). "Did the walk up the pathway inspire you just a little bit?" I received a few blank stares, so I continued: "Did you notice the tombstones on either side of you as you walked up the pathway?" I saw a couple of nods, so I said, "Walking up that pathway made me feel real lucky to be alive. I feel nothing right now but joy, and you should too, because it's not your name on one of those tombstones." They all began laughing, and I could literally see the tension start to ease. They were given a big reality check. They were experiencing a jackpot moment.

Do yourself a favour each and every day and pay attention to the numerous jackpot moments in your life and give thanks for the privilege and pleasure of experiencing such moments.

The Power to Feel the Love
(even when you don't feel like it!)

"The best cure for a reactive egotistical point of view is love and light." —Rosita

I have entertained the company of my ego on far too many occasions and as a result have found myself in situations that love would have handled differently. All because my ego's shout was louder than love's whisper. Ego's shout was saying, "But I'm right—they're wrong and I have to let them know at any cost." Sometimes ego's shout drowns out love, saying, "Let it go." Does this sound familiar to you?

I believe that many of the interpersonal disagreements or difficulties that we experience in the workplace, at home, or even with strangers often do not produce positive outcomes because we are egotistically reactive and not proactive. Ego reacts and goes for the jugular, and love waits and takes time to consider the best solution for all involved. Love prefers to handle any situation with a listening heart, respect, and regard for the other person's feelings. Love always aims for a win/win solution whenever possible. Love recognizes that reality is perception and that everyone has a different reality. Love takes time to understand.

When was the last time you encountered someone whom you considered to be difficult to get along with, or someone whom you totally disagreed with on an issue or the handling of a situation? How did you respond to this person or persons? Did love lead or was ego out of control?

We live in an ego-driven society where most people want to be in control, have the last word, be right, and—the big one—want to change people! This type of thinking sets up barriers to effective communication and resolve and will always make developing positive relationships difficult. The next time you encounter someone you consider difficult to get along with or someone you disagree with on an issue, approach it from this set of principles:

1. Don't try and change people; that is ego talking and saying, "I know what's best for you. If only you acted this way or responded this way we'd get along better." The bottom line is that people don't want to act like or be like you.

2. Treat people the way they want to be treated (the platinum rule), instead of the old adage of treating people the way you'd like to be treated (the golden rule). This is ego based and assumes people want to be treated the way you like to be treated.

3. Try to understand an individual's value system, which will indicate clues about why they believe the way they do, work and act in a certain way.

4. Tune into their channel and not just yours.

5. Speak their language.

6. Appreciate the fact that perhaps they have been brought to you or this situation for a reason, perhaps to teach you something about yourself. Teachers come in clever disguises.

7. Try to see people as different, not difficult. It only becomes difficult when you don't respect the difference.

8. Try to infuse laughter or humour into every situation. It is the shortest distance between two people.
9. Choose kindness over being right.

10. Feel the love! Let me explain this one. I belong to a volunteer group where members often get in a tizzy with each other over the tiniest things. I remember seeing one member becoming so agitated at another member that I could see steam coming out of her ears. So I approached her and said, "I know Karen annoys you, but why don't you stop seeing all the negative things about her and just see love?" She looked at me as though I was crazy, so I continued, "Every one of us, no matter how many faults we may have, is filled with beautiful love that is so powerful. So instead of seeing all the other stuff that is apparently upsetting you, why don't you look for and feel the love!" I had no idea this would have such a positive impact. Our club's unofficial motto is "Feel the love!" We use it to diffuse any negative situation. It has actually become quite humorous as we remind each other to feel the love and not let ego rule!

If we practice these ten principles on a daily basis, then it will be much easier to hear love's whisper and get along better with those people who work differently, think differently, respond differently, and look differently than we do. Let love rule!

The Power to Choose Happiness

"Happiness did not find me; instead, I found happiness." —Rosita

SIXTEEN SECRETS OF HILARIOUSLY HAPPY PEOPLE

1. They live like they are dying every second of the day.

2. They pray and believe in someone bigger than they are.

3. They practice kindness no matter how people treat them; they choose only to respond positively. However, they will not tolerate abusive situations or relationships.

4. They have great soul esteem and have daily "soulgasms"—the freeing of the soul to just be. Everyone needs to raise their soul esteem. A soulgasm is this deep feeling that you are alive, alert, and awake and you live like you're alive, awake, and alert.

5. They take time for quiet meditation and reflection.

6. They choose carefully who they are going to spend the majority of their time with. You don't usually see hilariously happy people hanging out with wet blankets.

7. They practice seeing humour in situations where others may miss it!

8. They count their blessings each and every day.

9. They capitalize on every opportunity to pay it forward.

10. They have found their soul mate and are deeply in love.

11. They have found their passion and are doing exactly what they were put on this planet to do.

12. They are great philanthropists.

13. They live in the present moment!

14. They choose to be happy.

15. They care deeply for their health.

16. They mind their own business, and they don't get caught up in second-hand stress.

The Power of "Ever-ready Me"

*"God could not use me in my state of slumber.
To do work for his kingdom, I had to be ready." —Rosita*

It's Sunday morning, February 20, 2011. I am getting ready to go to church, and suddenly I am emotionally impacted by a book I started reading the night before, entitled *Lioness Arising*. In it, author Lisa Bevere challenges women to discover the lioness within, to wake up and discover fresh passion, prowess, and purpose. She talks about how beautiful the lioness is when she arises from her slumber and how fierce and powerful she is. A force to be reckoned with.

As I am standing in front of the mirror, I hear this small voice inside of me say "It's time to awaken the lioness. It's time to hear her roar." I hesitated, but for only a few seconds and quickly I said out loud, "Yes, Rosita, it is time to awaken the lioness, she has been slumbering for far too long." I suddenly got this burst of energy, my face lit up, and I felt this great sense of strength overcome me. For a moment I felt like a superwoman, like I could take on the world and do anything I wanted to. I felt fierce, fabulous, and feisty. I spent the next few minutes reminding myself that I was now a lioness and it was now time to roar my way to success.

By 9:30 a.m., I was sitting in a church pew. The pastor began his message, which was entitled "Everready me." He challenged us as a congregation to live our life in such a way that people would want to approach us to ask us about the hope they see in us. He said people will especially want to know what it is that we hold on to, what the anchor is in our lives that gives us this hope during those difficult times. He asked us all to think about how we would respond to those questions. He followed up by asking if someone does approach us, are we willing and able to share this hope? I thought for a second that yes, I am definitely *willing*, but I had to think twice about the *able* part.

Prior to my encounter that morning, I had proclaimed myself to be in a deep slumber. And even at the point where I felt the lioness arising, it was not directly about serving the needs of others, or being an example to others, but rather, it was about my success. My first thoughts were, *how can I use this new strength to become more successful?* Clearly the lioness would fall back into slumber unless the awakening was about more than just me. I had to go back to the drawing board and really figure out why she was suddenly arising.

First and foremost I determined that the arising was actually a wakeup call, and the lioness was really just stirring. It was when the pastor spoke that the real awakening process started to happen. The pastor directed me back to the place where I truly believe God wanted me to be. He wants me to roar for his kingdom, not mine. He wants me to be my brother's keeper. He wants me to love the way he loves, walk with and care for the disenfranchised, care the way he cares, see the way he sees. He wants me to be his heart, hands, feet, ears, and light. He wants me to be willing and able to respond when someone asks, "What is the hope I see in you?" Wow, so God was awakening me so that I could be a blessing to someone else.

God uses us all in the most majestic and impactful ways, but this can only happen if we can humbly arise, awaken, and approach all that we do with his grace; understanding and remembering to do so for one reason only and that is to glorify his name, not ours. I know with my deepest conviction that my speaking ability is a God-given talent. I also know that God wants me to use it to glorify his name. Success is just the byproduct. So again, a much-needed reality check hit me over the head just to remind me that it's not about me. Rather it is about being a shining example of God's grace, love, and forgiveness and also an example of trust, hope, and obedience. The lioness is definitely stirring, and I do feel her awakening except with the revelation that she is going to be fiercer, more focused, bolder, and ferocious as she arises from the innermost being of my soul, at a new level where God can use me according to his will and not mine.

As I write this next paragraph, six days have passed and I have had time to reflect on my inner stirring since last Sunday. I feel good. I can feel a physical and emotional transformation. I feel like God is ready to take me to a new level of this journey he has me on. It's no accident that I purchased *Lioness Arising* by Lisa Bevere. Most people would describe me as an energetic, fearless, and fierce person, and so they would perhaps be a little surprised that I have described myself as not being fully awakened. What they don't know, however, is that you can have a false sense of being awake, in particular if this sense of being awake is ego or flesh based. The real awakening is God based.

Today I have committed myself to honouring the arising of the lioness within me by using the gifts God has given me to touch the hearts and souls of everyone I come into contact with, but this time from a God base not an ego base. It's not about me. I will use my gifts not to create success but rather to change the world for good. I think success will be the byproduct. And if my arising causes and stirs the roar in other people, then we can collectively roar and change the world. There is power in numbers. I can now respond to the question that the pastor asked on February 20, 2011, and my answer is this: yes, I am willing and able because the lioness is definitely arising and she is ready to do God's will.

The Power to Stay in Your Own Lane—Leadership 101

"Politeness is not an option, it is a requirement." –Rosita

I have had the distinct privilege and pleasure of leading numerous organizations through leadership challenges and have also had firsthand experience in leadership roles, and I have to admit, I have one minor—well maybe it's a major—pet peeve. Simply put, it's those folks who don't stay in their own lane. Let me explain: I have encountered many organizations with talent oozing from one end of the organization to the other. I am sometimes overwhelmed by the capacity that I see in so many individuals, from the top level right down to the guy or gal who cleans the bathrooms. But even with that much talent, issues still crop up, and the biggest issue I hear is that someone meddled in someone else's department or in their project. It was of no concern to them, they took over the project because they wanted all the recognition. They wanted all the "attaboys" (a new word from my husband's friend). In other words, all the pats on the back, you know, the words and gestures you use when your child does something wonderful and you want to encourage a repeat of the behaviour. Your child is most deserving of the attaboy or attagirl, whatever the case may be, but what's up with the grownups in the workplace still looking for theirs? Is there a "look at me" frenzy going on? Adults needing ongoing validation, really? And will they stop at nothing to get it?

There is nothing that crushes team spirit faster than folks who drive in the wrong lane. In other words, the folks who meddle in projects that they are not qualified to do, or insist on helping out where their help is not needed, or who may further insist that they can do the job better. In the meantime, no one has given them the authority to do so. Their arrogance just continues to feed them with egotistical delusions that things just cannot get done at a level of excellence without their Midas touch. Can you believe it?

Here's the deal: make sure you know what your talent is and use it to the best of your ability to create excellence and build effective relationships. Do it in a kind and spirited way and do it in your own lane. Most of us know the feeling of driving along the highway, minding our own business, when someone decides to cut over into our lane right in front of us with no warning, without affording us the courtesy of sig-nalling that they are coming over. As you know, when a car signals on the highway it means they intend to turn or come over into your lane. You have some warning, but when you don't, it can be dangerous because you are not prepared for their move into your lane. So whether it is on the highway or in the work-place, do us all a favour and stay in your own lane!

If you are going to go into another person's lane by interfering with a project they are working on, at least signal and let them know of your intentions so that they know you're coming over. When you signal or let them know your intentions, it builds trust. No one wants unnecessary surprises. On the highway, changing lanes without warning is a safety issue. In the work-place, it is a respect and common courtesy issue. And if respect and common courtesy is violated, it can cause havoc in the workplace.

Be respectful of the talents of everyone on your team. Don't meddle in the affairs or assignments of others unless you first simply ask, "Can I help you?" Don't take it upon yourself to cut them off and start leading the project yourself. Most importantly, don't hang around waiting for ways to get accolades. Just simply go along doing what's best for the team and the end results. The most successful teams are those who don't care who gets the credit; they just want to do their best and get the best results. Remember, leader-ship 101 is not about individual success but about the success of the team!

The Power to Sit Down and "Dummy Up"!

"In silence, wisdom speaks to me." —Rosita

I have a fun sister-in-law who has always has no problem suggesting that people should "just sit down" when situations get tense or stress levels go up. What she means by that is that we should just stop, take a deep breath, and think instead of reacting. I always have a great chuckle whenever I hear her speak those words of wisdom, and I have since added another suggestion to her great words of wisdom. Not only should we sit down during such times, but I think that we should also "dummy up" after sitting down. You see, a dummy can't speak, move, or think unless someone is pulling their strings.

I think the best stress reliever is to just simply sit down and silence oneself of all the external and internal dialogue and distractions. No thoughts, don't think, just go into the dummy zone for a few minutes. The dummy zone gives you a breather, a time to do nothing! It's a super mini retreat of absolute nothingness. I wonder how many of us could actually do that. When things get a little crazy, sometimes the best and only thing to do is to just simply stop! So you might be thinking *Okay, so I've stopped, I'm sitting down; I've dummied up for a few minutes, now what?* The answer, just continue doing nothing. You will need to stay in that state until you can think and act more rationally. I wouldn't dare give you a time frame. You will know when your engine has cooled down and when to proceed.

There is so much power in doing nothing. I can remember, when my children were small, that when they were quiet I'd ask them what they were doing. When they responded "nothing," it would make me nervous, so I would check on them. Sure enough, they'd be doing nothing. I of course thought that was ridiculous and never left them alone and would always challenge them by asking, "How can you do nothing?" I'd then try and get inside their heads and I'd say, "You can't be doing nothing. Even if you are not physically doing something, your mind is working, so what are you thinking?" Again, I would get "Nothing." At that time I just couldn't imagine anyone being in nothing mode, so I would continue on with the questions and my big lecture about how you have to be thinking about something...blah, blah, blah!!! My children would just look at me as if to say, "Why can't you get this, Mom?" And more importantly, why can't you leave us alone in our nothingness state!

Most of us don't realize just how powerful that state really is. What is this nothingness state anyway? My children at a young age helped me understand their definition of nothingness.

As adults we spend a lot of time thinking about the future, including things such as our health, finances, career, economy, death, taxes, retirement, etc. At the time, my children were too young to be spending time figuring out the future, so that was not a viable concern. They did not have all of that stuff racing around in their heads.

As adults we also spend a lot of time thinking about the past. The good and the bad times. At ages eight and eleven, my children did not have a past, no old landscapes holding them hostage; they only had right now. That would leave a lot of mental space for nothing. In fact, they were probably experiencing sheer bliss. They had, and still do, two loving parents, a roof over their heads, their own bedrooms filled with everything young boys their age could imagine, lots of fun family vacations, all their favourite foods in the kitchen, and really good family, neighbours, and friends. They had nothing to concern themselves about, and so there was a lot of space for "nothing." I have found that the majority of young children can only identify with the present moment—an art that most of us as adults are unable to do.

So it's the past and the future that uses up much of the head space in adults. And that impacts our present moment living. We respond to current situations based on our experiences from the past or our concerns about the future. As a result, we keep ourselves stressed to the max. Take a page out of my sister-in-law's book, and next time you are starting to feel the pressure of work, home, and life in general, find a big fat comfy chair and sit down, and then dummy up!

The Power to Juggle the Right Balls!

"If we don't prioritize those things in life that are important to us, someone else will." –Rosita

Last week I was delivering a session on leadership to a school board. I always like to bring the human caring aspect to every presentation I do, regardless of the topic, because the bottom line is that if we don't know how to care for ourselves and connect with people at the heart, most of our efforts will be futile. I told the audience that one of my greatest self-care strengths is the ability to prioritize those things in life that mean the most to me. I told them that every day I pick three things that absolutely mean everything to me in the world and I place them on my mental radar screen. They become the focal point around which all other things must be built. For example, my three picks today are my health, my husband, and my two sons, Joshua and Chris. So today I must ensure that I save enough energy to have quality time with myself, my husband, and my sons. Everything is secondary to these three priorities. Why? Because at the end of the day to me this is what really matters.

Those closest to me know that I live and breathe this model. On any given day, if the stress and activities in my life leave me depleted of enough fuel to attend to these things, then I will choose to give up another activity or work-related stuff so that the main thing remains the main thing in my life. My family will always come out on top, guaranteed! For me, this is an amazing self-care activity because when I get that right, it refuels me over and over again. I feel invigorated and on top of the world. As a result, I produce good results both on and off the job.

During break time at this particular session, a participant came up to me and said, "When you were telling us about your 'Pick Three' self-care plan, a thought came to mind." She continued by saying, "Your priorities are really your glass balls, and all the other stuff in life are plastic balls. What you've indicated is that you can't afford to drop the glass balls, namely your health, your husband, and your boys, right?" Wow! How insightful is that? She was absolutely right, and it was music to my ears that she got the message! Not only was she a wise woman, but she also handed me a great piece to include in my presentations on work-life balance!

Since that presentation, I have thought long and hard about the glass balls and just how powerful that participant's statement was. As life happens and people come and go, I know that the glass balls are the really special ones and I will do everything in my power to ensure that they stay intact and that those plastic balls don't get in the way and crowd out my glass ones.

I believe our relationship with the God we serve, our loved ones, and our health should be the balls we never drop. However, I witness glass balls being dropped every day as I travel around the country as a speaker and trainer and am privileged enough to hear intimate details of people's lives. It saddens me when I hear about heartache, separation, divorce, health issues, and relationship issues in the workplace. I wonder if things would have turned out differently had people understood which parts of their lives both on and off the job were just too delicate to not keep in focus. In other words, they dropped the wrong balls. Sometimes because it was the only thing left to do and sometimes because they were so busy with what they were doing, they didn't realize how precious the balls were in the first place until it was too late. It's hard to put a shattered ball back together again.

So please, pay attention to those glass fragile balls in your life. I have recently gone out and bought four glass balls, and I am going to have four names inscribed on them: Rosita, Norm, Chris, Josh. I will set them on my desk in a nice basket to remind me what really and truly matters. My ball will also have "Put God first" inscribed on it, along with "My health is my wealth." What do your glass balls look like, and in particular, what would you inscribe on the one with your name on it? It is a question we must all come to grips with if we are going to lead effectively at home, in our communities, and in the workplace.

The Power to Fulfill your Dreams

"Buried in the quietest place of your soul are your dreams.
You must visit this place often, and you must do it alone,
for only you, the keeper of your soul, can ignite the passion
and the will needed to bring them to life." —Rosita

I grew up in a small town in southern Ontario. The
population at that time was about 1,500 people. My
parents worked hard, but it was never enough to feed,
clothe, and care for fourteen children. Yep, you heard
me right: I have eight brothers and five sisters. I still
remember wondering each morning what I would pack
for my school lunch as the cupboards stared back at me
on most days with nothing to give. Our family was the
true definition of the working class poor. No matter
how much money seemed to come into the house, it
was never enough.

Growing up poor was one of the greatest gifts God
could have handed to me. It taught me to be happy
with who I was rather than with what I had. It rein-
forced the truth that my self-worth was not connected
to things, people, or money. Rather it was connected to
the one who breathed life into me. I learned at a very
young age that happiness had to come from within not
from external stuff. To this day, I live from the premise

that no matter how much stuff I surround myself with, in the end if joy isn't shouting from the very essence of my soul and from every corner of my home, then what's it truly all about? Now don't get me wrong, I don't have a problem with owning nice things and having money in the bank; in fact, I think I am deserving of it. However, my life is not centered around nor do I define myself by any of it. My self-worth is not determined by my net worth. My self-worth is determined by the one who created me.

As a youngster, poverty gave me the opportunity to use my imagination. I spent most of my time dreaming about what was possible, rather than on what I didn't have and how to bring that which I imagined into existence. The family purse may not have contained financial power, but the power of my ideas, imagination, and creativity was a great form of wealth for me and still is. My imagination gave me an unprecedented power to create and begin the manifestation process, although at such a young age I was not fully aware of what was unfolding.

From middle school right through to high school, I worked hard on my grades, held various odd jobs to make money, and spent my spare time watching those whose lives I wanted to emulate and imagining how I would make that happen. I had even pictured in my head the kind of neighbourhood I would like to someday live in, and I even knew the type of man I wanted to marry. I have told my husband on many occasions that I dreamed him into life. I knew education was key, and out of fourteen children, I was the first and the only child to graduate from university. I graduated in 1983 with a Bachelor of Social Work degree.

My childhood dreams of having a great education, a career, a fabulous husband, and being a mother have come to fruition. I have been married for thirty years to the man of my dreams. I have a job that I am passionate about, and my husband and I have raised two amazingly wonderful sons who have blossomed into the most amazing young men. I have some great women friends in my life who mean the world to me, and I am emotionally, mentally, physically, spiritually, and financially at peace. I give back to my community unconditionally, and I feel unspeakable joy dancing in the depths of my soul! My childhood dreams have come to fruition.

So today I sit in awe, and I feel fully awake and alive. The joy oozing out of my body has caused me to pause and reflect on how I was able to accomplish those goals and bring my life's dreams to fruition. I would like to share those thoughts with you in hopes that they may also encourage you and inspire you in your journey to bring yours to life as well. You may have read some of these tips in previous chapters, but I will repeat some of them so that you have them all in one place. Repetition is the best teacher.

❈ Have a deep and committed relationship with a power bigger than yourself. For me it is God, and his grace has covered me for as long as I can remember. My faith has been instrumental in every aspect of my life. My mom taught me at a very young age how important my relationship with God would be as I journeyed through life.

❈ Work hard and play even harder.

※ Be kind to everyone you meet. They may be the answer you need to elevate your life on both a personal and professional level.

※ Give generously. To whom much is given, much is expected.

※ Take care of your emotional, mental, and physical health; you are nothing without your health.

※ Build powerful relationships—they are fuel for life. Life is not a solo act, and you can't create success in a silo.

※ Be determined!

※ Don't allow other people to define you or write your life's script; that work can only be done by you.

※ Don't get in the ring with naysayers.

※ Carry your dreams close to your heart; be careful who you share them with.

※ Stay focused, hungry, and thirsty.

※ Arise early and go to bed early. The saying "The early bird catches the worm" is so true.

※ Hold on to your authentic truth—don't sell out on self!

※ Believe that you are deserving of all the goodness life has to offer.

✳ Professional development is a critical ingredient.

✳ Help others bring their dreams to life.

✳ Give daily thanks for your blessings.

✳ Believe that you can make it happen!

The Power of Spending Time with God

Today I woke up inspired to spend the entire day completely with God. No cell phone, no social media, no conversations with friends, just me and God. How amazing is that to actually devote an entire day to the architect of the universe, who also happens to be omnipotent, all powerful, omniscient, knowing all things, faithful, forgiving, and a host of other incredible characteristics too numerous to list. What a day this was going to be. It couldn't be that hard, right? Wrong! My brain is so wired to respond to the simplest of distractions that all the excess noise of daily living kept interfering with my time with God.

I started off by just meditating on the word and then sitting quietly in my living room waiting for God to speak to me or at least give me some direction on how the day should unfold. While I had a lot to say to God, deep down inside I knew today would be about me listening and not me talking non-stop. So I sat waiting, but I quickly learned that God will do what needs to be done in his time and not mine. I decided after a period of waiting (it really wasn't that long) that I should continue on with my daily routines but as I was doing them I would focus on really experiencing and feeling God's presence in everything that I would do throughout the day. I would ensure that God was in every detail of all my thinking and conversations. Again, the daily distractions had me off target on a few occasions when my mind would wander off, thinking about something that was most definitely not Christ-centred. So I'd stop and ask God for both help and forgiveness.

By mid-afternoon I decided to take a walk down by the bay front, a place where I don't usually have trouble focusing on God. I was remembering a really good experience I had last fall at this same bay front. I even recorded the experience in my journal. Let me share that page from my journal with you:

Sunday, October 9, 2011

> Nature to me is God speaking to us with the volume turned up to maximum. For example, yesterday on my walk near the waterfront in my community, I was overcome with this feeling of solitude and joy as I walked along this beautiful path filled with trees exhibiting fall at its best and a body of water that stretched the distance of the trail that whispered to me as soft waves splashed upon some small pebbles. I was in awe of the great artistry of the Creator. It was a picture perfect day.

> The water was the most beautiful shade of blue; the skies rolled out a carpet of beauty with the most stunning clouds. The fall colours spoke to me words that only my heart could understand. I snapped a few pictures along the way; I wanted to capture this experience so that I could hold on to it forever. I watched birds perched on rocks out in the water, sitting as quietly as if they too were experiencing the same flow I was. God is an amazing conductor; only he could get nature, the birds, and me all together in unison experiencing this time.

After walking another kilometre or so, I came across a huge rock sitting very close to the water under a tree—I decided to sit and really feast on God's creation and admire the work of his great hands. I sat staring out at the water and feeling a gentle breeze hit my face. A thought crossed my mind: I wish I could stay here forever. Everything was so peaceful and tranquil and rich with love that only a master's hand could have created. I watched as leaves fluttered from the trees into the water. As each one hit, I imagined that it was a part of my life that I needed to let go of. As each leaf hit the water I named it and then watched it being carried across the water by gentle waves. It was as though I was releasing it back to God. It was no longer mine.

It felt so good. I felt like I was being stripped of some emotional baggage I had been carrying for too long. The funny thing was that I didn't know I had any baggage until that moment during my quiet time with the Creator. I had no idea God would be speaking to me on that day. But he did, and how sweet it is when he does and we listen and we obey. When was the last time you let go and really allowed God some room in your life? It is so easy to get caught up in the daily affairs of life and to totally forget to connect with the one who makes all things possible.

I sat on the rock engaging with God for about twenty minutes, and then it was as though my chain fell from me. I got up so easily and continued my walk. I felt energized and compelled to pull out my camera and take some more shots of the magnificence that surrounded me on every side. I just couldn't get enough. On the drive home I realized that I had been down that same path so many times but today was different. I listened, I watched, I really observed. I took time for God and he took time for me. On previous walks, it was about the exercise, how far I went, how fast I walked, and whether or not I'd make it home before "Dancing with the Stars." On this particular Sunday afternoon, it was all about me and God. He invited me to walk with him as I am sure he did on previous visits, but this time I embraced his presence and we walked and talked. When we listen, he truly does speak words of wisdom into our hearts and souls! That is one Sunday afternoon walk I will never forget.

I will never forget that day as I truly heard God speak to me over and over again. Today as I began my stroll down the same path, I again felt the presence of God. While I did get some great exercise, I also took the time to listen and see what God wanted me to see. The sun shone brightly in my face, reminding me of the importance of the light and how God wants me to be the light. The beauty that surrounded me reminded me that we all have such incredible beauty, which often is hidden by the wear and tear of life. But we can trade those ashes for beauty. I found myself stretching my arms out as if taking in and accepting all that God had to offer me. I came across a park bench tucked behind some trees but directly in front of a huge body of water. To my surprise, the bench was empty, so I went over and sat down. I couldn't believe how quiet it was and how beautiful and vast the lake was. Beyond the lake stood beautiful developed greenery. I could have sat there all day, and I should have, but it's really hard to give myself permission to just sit and enjoy the moment. A voice inside my head (I think it was the voice of guilt) kept saying, "You need to get up and walk, you need the exercise," and so off I went. And as I walked away, I continued enjoying my beautiful surroundings and continually gave thanks for the privilege of such amazing moments.

I have now committed to spending more and more time with God each day and to really identify with the fact that the Holy Spirit lives in me and that I need to walk, talk, think, and behave like someone who is one with the Holy Spirit. Not an easy task, but I am determined to work on it every day for the rest of my life. Even today God spoke to me; he said, "Be the light, trade your ashes for beauty, take time to listen in solitude." The vastness of the waters reminded me of how big God is and how minute I am in comparison. I am sure there were more messages in that walk, but I, like the rest of the human race, allow the ego and noisy chatter and distractions to take away from the thing that matters the most, a deep and committed relationship with the one who created us all. May we all move one step closer to this amazing source available to us all every day.

The Power of Optimal Performance

"I need to be my best in order to give my best." —Rosita

My twenty-year-old son Joshua, who has taken quite an interest in health and fitness, has asked me on a couple of occasions, "Mom, are you eating for performance or pleasure?" He would then tell me how important it is to eat food that would allow me to be at peak performance every day. Although initially I didn't make much of it, I gradually began to digest the simple truth about what he was saying. Food does impact our performance. I started paying closer attention to the impact foods were having on my energy level, mood, and ability to think more clearly. He was so right. I feel so much more alive, awake, and alert, and I am thrilled to say that my weight started dropping. Why? Because every time I am ready to put something in my mouth, I hear my son saying, "Performance or pleasure?" I do have to admit, though, that I do sneak in a few pleasure foods once in a while. (Hope Josh doesn't read this!)

His words are deeply ingrained in my heart and soul and have had an even greater impact than he knows; not only do I consider his remark when I am feeding my physical body with food but also when I am nourishing my soul, emotionally, mentally, and spiritually. There is a lesson in Joshua's statement for all of us, in particular when we consider how we feed our bodies beyond the physical aspect and consider the emotional, mental, and spiritual aspect of our lives as well. How do we nourish ourselves in that realm? Is it coming from the "dumpster"—via gossip, negative conversations, wrong TV shows, music that belittles, soap operas, etc.? If so, this is not the living or performance food but rather it is dead food, for it has no nutritional value. If you put trash in, then you get trash out. We are not trash receptors, so our nourishment, emotionally, mentally, and spiritually, should come from the good stuff.

If we are to become everything that God wants us to be, we need to perform at our highest level. We need to think like the eagle and soar high above all the rubbish. Eagles pursue living food while the buzzards, vultures, crows, and even the chickens eat dead food. You have to make a choice: do you soar with the eagles of life or hang with the chickens? If you want to soar, then you have to stay out of the dumpsters and stay focused on the good things in life. If you are around negative people, excuse yourself and get up and leave the situation. If negative commercials or programs come on TV—change the channel. That's the beauty of owning a remote control. Don't listen to music that is belittling to women or to another race, etc.

We are the temple of the most high, and it is our job to keep it clean. Tomorrow morning when you wake up, employ these simple suggestions so that you fuel yourself for performance throughout the day:

> ✳ For emotional performance, continuously repeat the following mantra throughout the day: "Today I get to choose how I am going to

respond to every situation that comes my way, both on and off the job. I will choose the positive route because I am fuelling for performance. Pleasure will be the byproduct of making this choice."

✳ For physical performance, exercise at least twenty minutes each day and fuel your body with foods that energize you. Pleasure will indeed be the byproduct, due to the great way you will feel after following a strict regimen.

✳ For mental performance, incorporate the two suggestions above on a daily basis, coupled with a determination to put first things first each day. Figure out your number-one priority. If you have three or four, then you won't maintain your focus. It is hard to maintain mental focus with all the distractions we are faced with each day, so we must make a daily game plan. The power of focus is what separates those who are good from those who are great. Great mental focus can lead to incredible success.

✳ How badly do you want it? How badly do you want to perform at your best? If you are not hungry at the core to make these changes in your life, they won't happen. You have to be so hungry that nothing will stop you from making it happen. Good luck! You can do it—you've got the power!

The Power of Hunger

"I constantly hunger for more than what I was yesterday simply because I know there is so much more in me." –Rosita

At about the age of thirteen, my son Joshua had what could be described as a bottomless pit. This child ate nonstop around the clock. And the more he ate the more he wanted. I remember watching him have a meal and then run to the sub shop for a foot-long sub. I used to think, "Oh the joys of youth, to be able to eat that much food and not gain a pound." At the age of twenty this young man is still slim and trim. He was obviously burning off the calories. My point, however, is not about his weight but rather about his hunger. Joshua was hungry because he was growing and his body needed the nourishment. He was hungry because his body was screaming "I need more. I am developing and growing." As Joshua fed his body he felt happy, awake, alive, and alert. I am sure it impacted the results he was having in the various activities he was involved in and on his academic achievements.

As adults we grow hungry too. If we feel a great hunger to accomplish a goal or a dream, that can be a really good thing. But if the hunger occurs because we feel depleted emotionally, mentally, or spiritually, this can be concerning. If our well becomes empty in those areas, we must be careful how we fill the void. We often search outside of ourselves to fill this emptiness. People have been known to turn to food for emotional comfort or to alcohol, bad habits, or bad choices. We can also fill this void with bad friendships or intimate relationships. Not nurturing your emotional, mental, and spiritual void can lead to negative consequences.

Unlike the hunger Joshua was experiencing, or that hunger associated with accomplishing a goal, task, or dream, the hunger caused by emotional, mental, and spiritual emptiness can only be filled from the inside. There are many reasons why this emptiness occurs. The main reason, however, in my humble opinion, is because we become too distant from God. We start filling our lives with stuff that is so inconsequential compared to that which God can provide for us. We become distracted, and instead of going inside ourselves to find peace, harmony and fulfillment, we look externally. So the further we get from God the deeper the thirst and hunger will be.

If we are going to fill this void, we must place the burdens that are causing this disconnect from God firmly in his hands and rely on him to deliver us from the hunger. A bottomless emotional, mental, and spiritual pit can leave us wandering aimlessly through life with no sense of direction or purpose. It is difficult to set goals and accomplish our goals if we are feeling defeated emotionally, mentally, and spiritually. Take time each day to ensure that you are filling your pit with all the blessings, love, and self-care required to produce good results.

The Power to Paint Your World *Beautiful!*

"If a picture paints a thousand words, then why can't I paint you?" This is from a song by a group called Bread.

What is the picture you wish to create? You are the artist, the canvas is blank; dip your brush into the fountain of life and begin your creation. Introduce the world to fabulous you! The only prerequisite is that you must paint from the present moment; the canvas does not invite strokes from the past or the future, which is yet to be unfolded. Stay in the present moment, and let the magic begin. Paint from the essence of each heart beat, from the very core of who you are. Use your creative genius for inspiration. We all have creative genius inside of us. If you don't believe me, visit a kindergarten class. Paint your world fabulous because you are indeed incredibly fabulous in this present moment. Share with us your great passion for life.

What is it that is inspiring you at this moment? Paint your masterpiece with conviction, courage, and determination. *Bring to life the you that is God inspired*, and somewhere in your masterpiece add some strokes that would signify the type of day you are expecting to have right here and now. It should be congruent with the special you that the picture portrays. Now stand back and admire the great work you have done. How beautiful it must be to escape reality, if only briefly, to clearly paint the authentic you and the kind of day you are choosing to have.

Imagine what the world would look like if we all started taking responsibility for the direction of our lives and lived according to the picture we create for ourselves, instead of knowingly or unknowingly placing the paintbrush in someone else's hand to determine who we are and the type of day we will have. Would a great artist and painter like Picasso ever entrust his work to someone else while he merely stood on the sidelines watching as someone else attempted to paint his ideas, dreams, stories, or experiences? Absolutely not! An artist must paint what pours from his or her heart and soul because the inspiration, passion and creative energy must come from within.

Nobody has what Picasso had, and likewise nobody has what you have. You are one of a kind. The world will never again experience the incredibly and richly unique brand that you, Picasso, and others bring. Only once in a lifetime could such a beautiful array of awesomeness occur.

Picasso had to choose how and what to paint. He also had to determine the type of day he would have, as I am sure that the type of day he was having inspired his ability to paint. If you want to use your great gift as Picasso did each day, then start each day by mentally painting an outline of how you want your day to unfold and then colour it with all the great things you will be doing to make it an exceptional day! Do not allow anyone else to interfere with or tinker with that process. Come on, you can do it because you've got the power.

The Power to Shine On!

"I refuse to hide my light...
if it's too bright for you then go to another room." —Rosita

God has been good to me. He has placed in me the gifts of kindness, understanding, and love in great abundance, and of course he has blessed me with the gift of gab. If enough people would listen, I would talk 24/7. When you have been given such a gift, you must honour God by using it. We are giving back to God when we do so.

I have always had a great fascination for people: their stories, their struggles, their triumphs, and their passions. This excites me. I just simply love God's most precious creation, people. God has also equipped me with an abundance of energy. I have been asked on several occasions in my life if I take drugs! It is funny how some folks just simply can't understand why I have chosen to be a bright light for God, myself, and others.

I was told once that I should not let my light shine so brightly that people cannot see God's light. I spent months trying to figure out how to let God's light shine instead of mine, and then one day I had an aha moment when I realized that my light is God's light. His spirit lives in me, and the light that was shining through me had to be God's, light as there was no possible way that I could be feeling the kind of joy I was experiencing or having the kind of impact on others by my own accord. It was and still is God doing a good work through me.

When we are in relationship with God, walking in love and obedience with a forgiving heart, his love will shine through us. It doesn't mean that I'm perfect, as there is no such thing as perfect people, but I do serve a perfect God. Even with all of our imperfections, we are capable of shining. We are never to hide our light under a bushel because others are uncomfortable with it. We are all at a different place in our faith journey and we must always be respectful and supportive of each other. It is not our job to judge others. Let's leave that to God. Our job is to just reflect the light. Some of those lights will shine much brighter than others, but they all serve a purpose even if we as humans can't figure it out.

As we go through our day, let's remember who we are in Christ Jesus and let us be that beacon of light and hope to others who may find themselves in a season of fog or darkness.

Last year I was in Nova Scotia for a speaking engagement. I landed at the airport and decided to rent a car instead of having someone pick me up. I wanted to drive and see the great countryside I had heard so much about. Little did I know that by the time I landed that evening, the sky was growing dark, coupled with an extremely heavy fog. Everything in me said, "You should probably hail a cab"—it would be very expensive but much safer. Instead, I went against my better judgment and rented a car—big mistake, or so I thought. From the moment I got into that vehicle I couldn't see two feet in front of me. This was going to be a really tough drive. Would my GPS be my saving grace? I had estimated earlier that it would be a forty-minute ride. I had never travelled on those roads before, so I was not aware if the roads had twists and turns or whether or not it was a straight highway ahead. I had absolutely no idea.

So I started praying for light and guidance from the only true source of light. I was ever so thankful when I would see taillights from another car in front of me. It relaxed me and I didn't feel so lost and alone in unknown territory. But when the taillights would fade into thicker patches of fog, my panic button would go off again, although only briefly because I would remind myself to focus on the real light—the light that I knew would get me safely to the hotel. I found little comfort in the friendly voice on the GPS because while the directions were great, the visibility was really poor. As cars ahead of me continued to fade into even deeper patches of fog, I realized that I was alone with God. What more could I ask for? However as the fog thickened even more and the visibility worsened, panic set in and I had a hard time convincing myself that God would take care of me.

As I began praying harder, I noticed a car coming close behind me, and something at that moment became so clear to me: someone was now following me and was most likely dependent upon my taillights to guide them through the thick fog. Suddenly I felt this sense of responsibility that now someone was depending on me. I started to trust completely that God would indeed direct me to that hotel safely if I just believed. My faith would have a ripple effect because I would also lend a hand to someone else who was perhaps feeling a little lost and alone in the fog as I did initially.

The moral of this story is that we must have faith and keep our light shining, regardless of what is going on, because our light may be the guiding light that someone else needs at a time when we least expect it. I made it safely to my hotel room that night, gave a big sigh of relief, and thanked God for his mercy. I learned a lot about "the light" that evening. The car that was driving in front of me was a constant reminder that the light of God is always with me even when I cannot see it. That car following behind me reminded me that I must constantly let my light shine as a beacon of hope for all those I have the pleasure of meeting in this lifetime.

So, for the folks who think I should turn down my "joyometer," also known as light, understand this: the light that God gave me does not come with a dimmer switch. In fact, it doesn't come with a switch at all. This light is to be on all the time, every day, in everything that I do. For those of you who have been impacted by the light or walk in the light, you know the power of being driven by the light. Your light does not have to shine as brightly as mine or anyone else's. It is not how bright your light is, it's that you have one and that it's shining. Even a little match shines brightly in the dark, so embrace the light and *shine on!*

The Power to Let Jeannie out of the Bottle

I remember as a kid watching the show "I Dream of Jeannie." It was a story based on a captain and former astronaut who, while stranded on an island on a mission, discovered a mysterious bottle. When the captain opened it, a genie was released. The genie, whose name happened to be Jeannie, had been trapped in the bottle for some time. She was more than overjoyed about being released. The captain was eventually rescued and decided to bring Jeannie back with him to Florida. To demonstrate her gratitude, she promised to serve the captain. The storyline was centred on this beautiful woman with magical powers who lived in a bottle and could be summoned to do her master's bidding whenever she was called upon.

I was quite young when that show aired on television. I don't think it would be the hit today that it was back then. Can you imagine in the twenty-first century, a woman living in a bottle and only allowed to surface and utilize her gifts when summoned by her master? Activists would have a field day with this scenario, and so would I and the many women I have in my life. Are you kidding me?

If this is the case, why is that so many of us (in particular women) walk around with the genie in the bottle mentality? We forget about the amazing power we have, and we often depend on others to release the power in us and for us. Hello, only you can let the genie out of the bottle. We put a cap on our abilities, worthiness, desires, and potential. We admire the great qualities and abilities we see in others and sell ourselves short when it comes to our own. I say it is time to let Jeannie out of the bottle for good. Let the world experience her in all her radiance. My modern-day acronym for G.E.N.I.E. is noted below:

G—Greatness: the modern-day genie walks in her *greatness*—no one wants to follow ordinary, there are no books on being ordinary, and the media doesn't celebrate ordinary. One of the greatest handicaps you can inflict upon yourself is *ordinary*. You are extraordinary, and there is no duplication of any one single fingerprint. Every person is an original; hold yourself to a higher standard than anyone else expects of you. Greatness simply means that you become fully yourself by letting go of self-doubt, social myths, and the voice of naysayers. You know the ones who say, "You're too old" or "You're too young," etc. Pay no attention because remember, it is not your business what others think about you. Stay fully alive and connected to the power we all have within, and utilize that unique power to make a difference in the world.

Greatness doesn't mean that you need to do huge things. It means that whatever you do, you pour into it your complete being. Have you ever spent time with someone who has unleashed their greatness? It is so empowering and refreshing, not to mention inspirational. On a personal note, walking in my greatness became clear once I realized the gift God blessed me with and the impactful results I was witnessing when I started using my gift in an honourable way to make a difference.

E—Engaging: she is bright and articulate and has a very attractive aura about her. She always makes her presence known simply by just showing up in all her strength, beauty, and intellect. She is like a magnet, and she attracts great people and opportunities.

N—Noble: she has high moral qualities and ideals; she is trustworthy, and people know that they can depend on her for consistency, honesty, and for always taking the "high road."

I—Independent: she is self-assured, an independent thinker; she knows how to take care of herself.

E—Energetic: she believes in the power of self-care, self-awareness, and self-healing. Her first priority is to maintain excellence in health.

There is no way that a genie possessing the above-mentioned qualities could possibly be contained in a bottle, taking orders from a colonel. I would love to be the writer of a new twenty-first-century version of this 70s show because it would be called "Master, take a hike..."!

The world needs and deserves to experience the amazing gifts everyone has in their own unique way. And we need to experience them all the time, not just when someone gives us permission to do so. So to men and women alike, it is time to come out of the bottle on your own. Let the genie inside of you with all those amazing qualities impact you and the people around you. Let your greatness shine, don't be afraid of it. Once you have an appreciation of your greatness, you will become the most engaging and exuberant individual that you can be. Stay focused as there is no greater thrill than walking this path. And as you walk, your enchanting personality will naturally unveil itself and the world will experience your extraordinary exuberance, your amazing character, wit, and independence. Break the chains of that bottle right here and now by letting go of every excuse you've ever had that keeps you inside that bottle, and any other self-doubts or fears, and start living the life you truly deserve!

The Power of a Personal Mission Statement

"I have chosen to live my life in a way that is honourable to God. I have chosen to live my life with peace and love, and to express that love and peace to others. I have chosen to see only the good in others. I have chosen to spend my life elevating the lives of others, and showing through my actions that they have incredible worth and value. If I choose otherwise, then I am committed to taking the time to examine myself and identify what it is that I am lacking, in order to understand why and how it is connected to devaluing the worth of others. *Furthermore, I choose to make positive choices that will allow me to grow and make time for health and fitness and time for loving and nurturing relationships with my family, friends, and colleagues. Every day I will incorporate laughter into my daily routine."

February 25, 2005; *Revised February 21, 2012

I take great pride in making every effort to live this mission statement each and every day of my life. Those who know me well would say that, yes indeed, this mission statement is etched on my heart and soul and I wear it proudly. I wrote my statement in 2005 and revised it recently. The first section is the original statement. The core of it remains the same and probably

135

will not change. I have certainly changed and grown in leaps and bounds since 2005, but my personal mission statement, the thing that drives me every day, still remains basically the same. Why? Because it is rooted in authentic truth. It is how I have chosen to live my life, regardless of circumstances and regardless of the roads that life leads me down. The emotional, mental, physical, and spiritual landscape of our lives will be swayed by many factors, and so our personal mission statement keeps us centred. The additional lines that I included recently have always been lived out in my life, so I decided to include them as part of my statement because of their importance.

Have you drafted your mission statement? Do you realize the impact o f having one? A personal mission statement is sort of like a personal constitution or creed about how you have chosen to live your life—it's the billboard that screams, "This is my vision and values, my character and what I want to achieve." No two statements will be alike, and there is no wrong or right way to develop one. It can include as much or as little detail as you see fit. However, it is a good idea to keep it brief and concise so that you know it like the back of your hand. It becomes your moral compass, the criterion by which you measure everything else in your life. A personal mission statement can keep you focused and prevent you from flip flopping on your values and what you hold to be true on an authentic level during times of crises, upheavals, changes, and challenges. If you say "Yes" every day to your mission statement, you'll say "No" to all the other unimportant activities that would otherwise interrupt your day.

Below are some steps to assist you in developing your own personal mission statement. Please note that this is not something that you can do overnight; it will take a lot of writing and revising. It took me several weeks to feel good about the one I wrote.

- First and foremost, find some quiet time on your own (no phones, technology, or people), just you and a sheet of paper. Notice I said no technology. I want you to actually write your statement down; computers can be distracting.

- Go deep inside your heart and soul and connect with what really matters to you. Be honest; this is not a test. It's your truth.

- Ask yourself, "What do I want? What do I value? How do I want to be remembered?

- What will be my legacy?"

- Have fun writing from the heart. You will be surprised and pleased with the finished statement. In addition, you will be pleased to have a moral compass to guide you through life.

The Power to Stay Aboard the Change Train and off the Fuss Buss

"Change introduces you to the real you!" —Rosita

Staying aboard the Change Train simply means making the necessary adjustments to work with *what is* rather than with *what used to be.* The alternative to this is staying "stuck" in the middle of upheaval, changes, or challenges; staying focused on the negative aspects (real or imagined); and choosing to stay with status quo even though it no longer exists. I refer to this as being stuck on the Fuss Bus, a deadly mode of transportation that can lead to heart disease, immune system deficiencies, sleep disorders, psychological disorders, and the lists goes on and on. The impact of the stress associated with not moving forward can be detrimental, on both a personal and professional level.

So my question to you is, "What mode of transportation have you been travelling on?" The Fuss Bus or the Change Train? If you are on that Fuss Bus, we have to get you off of it because your health is taking a beating. Let's begin with what we need to do.

In regards to dealing with ongoing changes in the workplace, I don't believe that any kind of change strategy can work unless it contains these three key components:

1. Each employee must be willing to take responsibility for their role and response to dealing with the change. They must also be on a constant self-awareness journey and understand at the deepest level their authentic truth, as this is the foundation they will need to stand on when things get tough (and they will) because change will challenge their identity.

2. The leadership team must be communicating with staff on an ongoing basis. Communicate: "This is what is going to happen." Don't get married to timelines because change is unpredictable and things constantly change directions and hurdles can appear even within the best-laid plans. Communicate why the change is happening and what it will look like when they reach their goal. Explain how change will be monitored and measured.

3.The leadership team must ensure that there is a plan in place and resources available in order to successfully support both the organization and the people through the transitional period. Some of those resources might be one-on-one coaching, access to EAP programs, mentoring, and professional education.

The role of leadership during these crucial times cannot be underestimated. If leaders are not ready or prepared to help employees work through transition, then change will be viewed as an event rather than a process, resulting in insufficient support and difficulty accomplishing the required outcome. As well, leaders should never underestimate the amount of emotional and physical energy required to move through the change process.

Once these three key components are in place, we can then look forward to boarding the Change Train, the healthy mode of transportation. If you are willing to pay and ready to board this fast moving, ever-changing, constantly evolving Change Train, you must be willing to do the following:

1. *Digest the simple truths about change*—Change management is an oxymoron: you cannot manage change. In order to survive, organizations of the twenty-first century will constantly have to examine, re-examine, define and redefine their vision, mission, and direction.

2. *Understand that change cannot happen without transition*—Change puts us in a state of transition. There are two sides of transition: emotional and rational. The emotional side of transition deals with how people are responding to the change; it is the psychological transformation that people will go through as a result of the change. The loss that change brings can be difficult for many people; we must take time to acknowledge that loss. We can do this by honouring the past and celebrating the future ahead. The rational side of change deals with the actual organizational changes being implemented, such as a change to systems, policies, procedures, or technology. In many organizations, the rational side of change is often given the most attention, and we often neglect to deal with the emotional side of change that our people are experiencing. If we try to deal with change without addressing the emotional side of transition, we will set the organization and its people up for failure. Your human resources have to be cared for first and foremost.

Often employees are dealing with possible changes occurring in their lives outside of the workplace as well. As a result, any change occurring in the workplace can add to an already overworked and stressful life. Change, regardless of whether or not it is work related, means that we must learn to deal with a new reality. Remember, reality is perception, so it will be different for each individual. Everyone will move through the process at their own pace; we must be respectful of that.

When I deliver sessions on change, I always share the following story so that people truly understand the psychological transformation happening to employees on a personal level and its impact.

When my son was about nine or ten, his friend from down the street gave him a blue piggy bank. This bank did not have the little piece you could take off that would release the change. It was uniquely made, and the only way to get the money out was through that very small slot at the top. The friend assured my son that he would not be able to get the money out, and this was a sign of how long the friendship would last. I thought it was touching. However, a few years later I heard my son in his room shaking the piggy bank. When I asked what he was doing, he said, "I am trying to get money out so I can buy something." I just smiled as he continued to shake the bank. Every once in awhile I would hear a shout of joy as a coin came tumbling out of the piggy bank. It took a little while, but eventually my son accomplished his mission and came out of his room with a hand full of change.

As I watched this process, it reminded me of the emotional transition we go through. My son had to keep shaking that bank until something of value came out. This is what happens to us during transition. The shaking process is the psychological transformation we go through in the midst of change. We will feel as though we have been shook up, but the good news is that at the end of it all something of value always comes out. For example, when we learn a new skill, we learn something new about ourselves and tap into knowledge that may have been laying dormant for a very long time. Don't be afraid of the shaking process—something good always comes out in the end. Be open and ready to receive the blessings.

3. *Develop an individualized self-care plan or safety net.* It must be practical, simplistic, and one that you can apply on a regular basis. As mentioned earlier, change requires a tremendous amount of energy and motivation.

4. *Digest the simple truth about the twenty-first century workplace:* organizations cannot continue to replicate practices of yesterday to deal with solutions of today. We need to re-think, use our imagination, and be creative and innovative. Do not define yourself by your job description; you are so much more. Do not ask, "What am I getting," but rather "What am I becoming?"

If you can integrate the knowledge outlined in these four important steps into your daily routine, coupled with a willingness to take responsibility for your role in the change process, and if the leadership team is committed to effective communication, providing the proper resources and paying attention to the emotional side of transition, then you should be able to capitalize on all of the opportunities that do exist in the midst of the reality of change.

The Power of the Ruby Slippers

"All roads lead back to self." —Rosita

As a child, I was always fascinated with the movie The Wizard of Oz, and I watched it several times. My favourite part was the ending, because Glinda the good witch would advise Dorothy to click her heals and think, "There's no place like home." I would feel my heart race with the excitement of knowing Dorothy would soon be back home in Kansas with those she loved. I really didn't like much else in the film; I just wanted to see Dorothy returned safely home. Each time it happened I cried. I knew the ending would always be the same, but none the less it always ended in tears for me. I will never forget the power in those red ruby slippers.

I am now the proud owner of a pair of Dorothy's ruby red slippers. When they arrived in the mail, I nearly fell over because they looked exactly like the slippers I remembered Dorothy wearing. For a moment I was taken back in time to that moment when she clicked her heels three times and everything changed. The red shoes have become a huge part of my fashion statement. Not a physical fashion statement, but an emotional, mental, and spiritual statement.

The ruby shoes are a constant reminder of how important it is to go home—not a home of bricks and mortar, but the home that is the keeper of our heart, soul, and dreams. Many of us have strayed from our real homes. Like Dorothy, we are trying to make it to the Oz. Dorothy needed to meet the Oz because she was told that he could help her get back home to Kansas. The Oz refused to do so unless she killed the wicked witch and brought her broom to him. Dorothy finally realized that she didn't need the Oz to get home.

Many of us are searching desperately to find our way home—a way to find peace, joy, and happiness for our internal homes. So we search aimlessly, hoping our Oz will have or be the answer. We search for the Oz who can provide more money, bigger houses, or better jobs to satisfy this internal hunger, and we often become disillusioned when it doesn't. Like Dorothy, there is a price to pay if we look to the Oz to fill this gap. Sure, the Oz of more money or the Oz of more real estate, better jobs, and prestige will give us a temporary fix, but I say click the heels of your heart and "Go to your bosom, knock there, and ask your heart what it doth know" (William Shakespeare).

I call it "heart intelligence," which is guidance from God. We are all worthy of the niceties of life; we just need to be sure that we have joy from a deep place already inside of us so that we don't look to the external things to bring us internal joy and happiness.

Yes, the yellow brick road can lead us to a lot of things; we just have to be sure that the price we are paying is not impacting our health, our relationships, and who we are at our core in a negative way.

The Power to Give!

The joy and excitement of giving often happens in those moments when you least expect it. At the end of one of my presentations, a kind lady came up to me with a small package wrapped in tissue paper and said, "This is for you. I really want you to have it." I was about to open it when she said, "I'd prefer if you opened it later in private. I don't want it to be a big deal." I obliged and thanked her profusely for a gift I hadn't opened.

When I arrived at the destination of my next presentation, I remembered the package, so I went through my briefcase to find it. When I opened it, my jaw dropped. It was a beautiful necklace with several crystal hearts. It had a note attached that read, "You have captured my heart. Wear this necklace knowing that you have touched many hearts." I was deeply touched. I had sat with this lady during lunch and had admired her necklace, and now here I was holding it in my hand. I quickly placed the beautiful necklace around my neck and wore it proudly to my next session. As soon as I walked in, I received several comments on how beautiful the necklace was. I told the audience how I had acquired it. They thought it was a beautiful story. I decided that this would be my "speaking necklace" and that I'd wear it to every engagement and share how I received it.

A few weeks later I was presenting to a group of Algonquin College employees. I wore the necklace to that engagement and shared how the necklace came into my ownership. At break time, one of the members of that group shared a powerful story with me and I felt touched. I felt with everything inside of me that I should pass this necklace on to her because she had impacted my heart. So after break, I explained this to the audience and took the necklace off and handed it to this particular woman I had spoken with at break. She was very surprised and overwhelmed. I told her I wanted it to now become the travelling necklace and that she too could pass it on when the right moment came. It was a very special moment. On my drive home I felt a little sad that the necklace no longer belonged to me, but I felt in my heart it was the right thing to do.

Fast forward a week or so later, and this is the email I received from the college:

> *Hello Rosita. Hope you had safe travels back and have big plans to celebrate Canada Day!*
>
> *You have no idea the size of ball you started to roll when you handed over the travelling necklace to Janice…*
>
> *Here is a link to the story featured on our employee intranet today…You may recognize something familiar?*
>
> http://myalgonquin2.algonquincollege.com/articles/anno uncements/xiaosi-ren%e2%80%99s-will-be-featured-on-cbc-during-canada-day/comment-page-1/#comment-1534
>
> *You will most likely remember seeing Xiaosi at the session. Well, after you left, she asked to speak to the group and thanked us all profusely for helping to build her confidence. She then proceeded to tell us*

about her great experience at Algonquin College...She was so happy with your presentation, she said, and she had us all in tears...What a special moment that was.

At the end when we gathered for our group picture, Janice felt it was appropriate to "already" hand over the precious travelling necklace...to VIP Xiaosi!

What a remarkable and memorable retreat this has been! Thought I'd better let you know...

We have received only positive comments about your keynote, Rosita—you have truly found your calling!

Happy Canada Day!

Val

p.s. Here is the link to our pictures:

https://picasaweb.google.com/ValSayah/AlgonquinSupport AdministrativeStaffRetreat?authkey=Gv1sRgCL— gOqA443P0AE#

Words cannot convey how deeply touched I felt receiving that email message. I had no idea that the necklace would have had that kind of impact. WOW! Now I felt compelled to let Mary Ellen know what had happened to the beautiful necklace she had given me. I felt concerned that she might ask about it one day, and so I decided to email her and tell her what had happened; the following is her verbatim response:

Your story has touched my heart. Wow, that is such a warm story...you see I work also with newcomers coming to Canada, and sure enough, my necklace is now around another newcomer. This speaks volumes to me as that heart resembles my love for my granddaughter Megan...a love that goes so deep that it is hard to comprehend...I know now

*that each person who wears that heart necklace will
be carrying Megan with them in their lives...this is
so deeply touching...I am brought to tears...you and
I have connected in a way that perhaps very few
people ever will...I am blessed to have met you and
shared my "forever in my heart Megan" necklace
with you and wherever it may travel!*

After receiving Mary Ellen's email, I phoned her to
ask about Megan, as I felt there was something missing.
What I learned was that her granddaughter has mito-
chondrial disease and Mary Ellen had purchased the
necklace one day while out walking at a mall because
the heart was symbolic of her love for Megan. She said,
"I am glad you passed it on so that everyone will have
a piece of Megan."

Again, a huge WOW! What in heaven's name had I
done with this necklace? It was having a roaring
impact. I had absolutely no idea this would happen. I
was witnessing the power of a simple act of kindness
and its rippling effect.

In July 2012, a year after the date that I did my presentation for Algonquin College, I received yet another
email from Algonquin College:

Hello Rosita,

*I hope you are doing well and enjoying your
summer. Well, your necklace has been around for
some exciting events in people's lives here at
Algonquin College, and we wanted to let you know.*

*The last you heard, I believe, was from Ginette,
who had received the necklace from Xiaosi, who had
become a Canadian citizen fairly recently last year
and was invited by the powers that be to attend the
Canada Day celebrations last July 1 on Parliament*

Hill when Kate and William were here. She had front row seats and met Kate and William all while she was wearing the "Travelling Necklace." In April of this year, Ginette was heading to Toronto to see Oprah, which has been a dream of hers, and Xiaosi gave her the necklace to wear at the Oprah show. I saw Ginette on TV out of thousands of people, and she had the necklace on!

Two weeks ago today we were back at the Glen House Resort near Gananoque, Ont. for another Support Staff Retreat. Ginette brought the necklace with her and on the first day presented it to Rena for running and completing the Boston Marathon. What a feeling that must have been for Rena to do this.

Rena, being Rena, was very shy about the whole thing and did not feel she deserved it, but she certainly did. Later on in the retreat, Rena passed the necklace on to Jessica, who is getting married next month (August) and was one of the organizers for the Support Staff Retreat this year who worked very hard in making sure everything went off without a hitch, which it did. Our best wishes and thoughts will be with Jessica on her special day next month.

During this time at the resort, my daughter-in-law went into labour on Wed., June 27, which is the day we arrived at the resort, and Thurs., June 28, at 10:30 a.m., our first grandchild was born. A boy. His name is Jaxon and he weighed 8 lbs. 15 ounces and was 22 1/2 inches long. It was a real fiasco during this time as many of our cell phones would not work at the resort, but somebody had a Blackberry phone that worked and I was able to borrow it to be reachable by my family and so I could call them. When I actually found out he had arrived, we were out on the St. Lawrence River on a lunch cruise from Gananoque. Everyone on the retreat knew what was going on during the whole time and kept checking in with me to find out what was happening. When I received the call on the boat that he had arrived, I yelled loud enough that they could hear me on shore. The staff on the boat gave me a glass of wine to celebrate, which was very nice of them, and there was a lot of hugging going on! On Friday before we left the resort, Jessica presented the necklace to me at the end of our morning session and thanked me for including them in my special event. It sure brought tears to my eyes. I wanted to drive the bus home but they would not let me. Something about safety and speeding!

Attached you will see my precious "event" and I am wearing the necklace. We will keep it going as a tradition for the next person in the college who has that special moment or even if it is for someone who needs a lift at a certain time in their life to know they have a whole bunch of people supporting them.

Thank you for passing your necklace on and starting this Algonquin College tradition!
Judy

So there you have it: the power of kindness and how far it can expand and the number of hearts that can be touched in doing so. I look forward to continually receiving updates on the travelling heart necklace, and each time I do, I will be reminded to say a prayer for Megan and for her grandma, Mary Ellen, who have started something beautiful amongst friends and strangers alike!

The Power to Move to a New Neighbourhood

One of the greatest joys of maturing on an emotional, mental, and spiritual level is that you grow tired of the same old neighbourhood; in fact, you actually become uncomfortable and emotionally drained because you have outgrown every aspect of it. And so, you make the choice to move to another neighbourhood. When you find the courage to make that move, it is the most surreal and beautiful experience ever! Now I am not talking about moving from a neighbourhood with houses made of bricks and mortar, but rather I am talking about the emotional and mental neighbourhoods we all choose to live in.

I will never forget the day I realized that I had made a huge emotional, mental, and spiritual move. I was sitting with a group of friends, and they began talking about a particular situation that was not very positive. As they were chatting, I just sat there and my mind escaped to somewhere else as they continued on. Suddenly one of my friends asked, "Rosita, what do you think?" and without hesitation, I said, "I don't, because I don't live in that neighbourhood anymore." They all looked at each other, then at me, and asked, "What do you mean?" I said, "I have moved on from those kinds of conversations a long time ago. I don't participate in negative conversations anymore. Emotionally and mentally I am now in a new neighbourhood." To this day I don't know where those words came from, but I am so happy to be in my new place.

You see, there was a period in my life where I would have engaged in that type of conversation but not anymore. I've had an address change emotionally, mentally, and spiritually. I have matured, which means I now choose to make the right decisions that I need in order to get that which I desire in life. Now, at the age of fifty-two, my desire is simply for unbridled health and happiness. The choices I will make will determine if that desire actually comes to fruition. As I consider the future and what it has to offer, I realize that in order to capitalize on all the goodness that awaits me, I must maintain my mental capacities, my physical abilities, and my emotional and spiritual capacities so that I can someday be the best grandmother in the world, be cheering from the crowd when my sons get their degrees from university, and crying with joy when they stand at the front of a church someday as they watch their beautiful brides come down the aisle.

Just thinking about all of those potential memory-making moments releases a passion and determination to care deeply for my health. What amazing moments to look forward to as a mother. And even more importantly, I also want to make great decisions about my health so that my sons don't have to spend the best years of their lives taking care of me because I have not cared for my mental or physical health. My husband and I have worked hard so that our children can have an even better life than what we have had. They deserve to live life to the fullest and cash in on the abundance of opportunities life will offer them. I don't want to have that interrupted because they have to care for parents who chose not to care for themselves when they should have.

Choosing the right neighbourhood to live in will increase the likelihood that I will not be dependent upon my children but will instead celebrate on a regular basis their successes along with my own. Again, it all comes down to choices.

Here is an example of a choice I recently made because a voice in my head kept reminding me of how I want to live my life as I grow older with my children. I was driving into a parking lot of a grocery store, and as I was turning down an aisle to find a parking spot, another driver was coming from the opposite direction, leaving the parking aisle I was turning into. As I was coming closer to the vehicle, I could see that the driver was quite upset, so I rolled down my window and asked if she was okay. She looked at me in anger and said, "Couldn't you have waited? Can't you see I am trying to get by?" Wow, I was surprised as it looked as though there was plenty of room for her to go by. She continued ranting, and I said to her in a very calm voice. "Hmmm, to me it looks like you have room to move forward, you should be okay." She snapped back very quickly and said, "Why don't you move?" I took a deep breath smiled and said, "Would you like me to move instead?" She screamed, "Yes!" and I smiled and said, "Okay, but before I do, I have something to say to you. I love you and so does God." This seemed to anger her more as she replied, "Oh great, a crazy lady." I drove to my spot, got out of my car with a big grin, and felt like a million bucks on the inside. As I walked through the grocery store with a big smile on my face, my inner voice was saying, "Good for you, your health is your wealth." I chose in that situation not to give my health away, and

I also chose not to visit the old neighbourhood. About ten years ago, I would have been compelled to get out of my car and give that lady a piece of my mind, but not anymore. I simply don't live there anymore. I don't let my ego take front and centre stage anymore.

When I returned home and told my son Chris about the incident, he replied, "Good for you, Mom, you killed her with kindness. Why should you be responsible for her bad mood? That lady was looking for a fight, and you didn't bite." Chris was absolutely right. Many of us, however, have a tendency to fight back because our ego becomes wounded. Our fragile egos can get us into a lot of trouble unless we choose otherwise.

Think about the things you are looking forward to in the coming days, months, and years and ask yourself if you are doing all that you can possibly do right now, in relation to your health, to increase the likelihood of your participation in whatever that might be. We take our health for granted, but if we really want the best from life right now and for the future too, we must focus on doing the right thing all the time. And if you can't, try moving to a new neighbourhood.

The Power of the Pit Stop

According to Wikipedia, in motorsports, a pit stop is where a racing vehicle stops in the pits during a race for refuelling, new tires, repairs, mechanical adjustments, a driver change, or any combination of the above. I am always amazed at how quickly the changing of tires and refuelling takes place. I am not a big race car enthusiast, but on a rare occasion when I have caught a glimpse of it on TV, I was more impressed with the how quickly the cars were serviced at the pit stops than the actual races. I was also very impressed with the dozens of people who were a part of the race team. Timing is critical, and everything seemed so well calculated and planned. I understand that the race cars are usually out of the pit within ten seconds. Every second counts in a race, so fast pit stops are important. Races are often won or lost in the pit.

How often do you take a pit stop from this fast-paced race called life? We spend hours on this track called life, and because the pace is so fast and so hectic, every one of us could use a pit stop or two throughout the day. A time to get realigned, refocused, readjusted, and refuelled. But like race car drivers, if this is going to happen effectively, we need to ensure that we purposely plan it and surround ourselves with the resources and the right people to make sure it happens. Otherwise the pit stop can turn into a "pit flop." A pit stop is obviously for a very short duration. A pit flop, on the other hand, can extend over a much longer period of time and can come with very negative consequences.

Sometimes the reality of life gets the best of us all and we struggle to balance our time between work and home; in doing so we sacrifice our health. As a result, those daily pit stops are forgotten and placed on the back burner, so to speak, as we work our way through all the other priorities on our to-do list. However, when reality sets in and our health starts to decline and the stressors eat away at our psychological and physical health, we attempt to fit our daily pit stops back into our lives again. Unfortunately, what happens at this point is that the pit stop becomes a pit flop.

Let me explain: if we are making a pit stop and the stressors we are carrying are so heavy that the brief refuelling is not enough, we will extend our stay (defeating the purpose of a pit stop) because we just don't have the energy to get up and go—we need more! Now the pit stop that was meant to be for a short period of time has now turned into hours, days, weeks, months, or perhaps even years. We have fallen deep into the pit flop! The stressors were just so huge that we need more than a pit stop; we decide to just flop. Our energy levels have been depleted.

It can be a dangerous game if we stay in the pit too long. Race car drivers can't afford to stay in the pit for any longer than a few seconds. For us regular folk, the pit stop is a good idea because we can all use refuelling at certain periods in our lives. The problem arises when we stay in the pit too long. When this happens, we sink deep into a pit flop. This can be a very dark and dreary place. We start out with great intentions but become caught up in all that is going on in our lives; we start to drown ourselves in the reality of what is going on to the point that it takes hold of us at such a deep level that we become captive and unable to move forward at a reasonable pace.

The solution then is to recognize that when our emotional, mental, and physical tanks are starting to lose fuel, we must make the stops earlier before we reach the burnout stage. If we do, we will increase the likelihood of our ability to operate at a level of excellence in everything that we do.

The Power to Sink Ships!

"I will guard my tongue and only allow it to speak in a way that builds up and does not tear down." —Rosita

I am sure that we are all familiar with the old adage "Loose lips sink ships." I heard those words come from my mother's mouth one too many times, but I am guilty of having sunk a few ships during my time here on earth, and regrettably so. Yet on a daily basis I still remind myself, "Rosita, do not respond," and my ego says, "But," and before I know it, another ship goes down.

Of course, I use the excuse, "Well, I'm only human" or "Maybe I am just too tough on myself," or "Perhaps what I said wasn't that bad." But my heart tells me another story. It says, "Rosita, if you are feeling that kind of guilt, then you've probably said something you shouldn't have said." The lesson learned is this: speak kindness into other human beings, think warm thoughts, and wish nothing but the best for everyone you meet. Yes, even if you don't like them. Perhaps the most important lesson of all is that we don't have to say anything. Perhaps we should practice keeping our mouths closed for a change. We don't have to judge every action or behaviour or comment on everything we hear from others. Sometimes the best response is simply no response.

Imagine how beautiful the world would be if each of us spent our time building people up instead of tearing them down with our insecurities, negative attitudes, and stressed-filled emotions.

Why do we have a need to comment on everything, tell someone else's story, and share something that we know we shouldn't be sharing, or just simply be mean to others? From what place do such actions come from? Why would anyone have a need to engage in such behaviour?

If you are guilty of sinking a few ships yourself and need answers to these questions, lift your head up from this page as you will not find the answers here. Find a quiet place alone and start soul searching and asking for guidance and forgiveness if you feel you need to be forgiven. I remember in university being such a talker that my peers started calling me "mighty mouth." At the time I thought it was funny, but I now realize that a mighty mouth can carry mighty powerful words, which can influence and impact in a mighty powerful (positive or negative) way.

When we start our powerful engines each day (our tongues), let us ensure that we fuel them with constructive wisdom, knowledge, and love. The fuelling starts at the heart and flows to the tongue. Take care that your heart is at peace, and ensure it is not filled with resentment, disappointment, frustration, anger, etc., as this is what will flow to our mouths and eventually to all of those we come into contact with during the day. It is not fair that others should have to bear the brunt of our unresolved issues of the heart.

We can only change ourselves, not other people, but we can certainly influence others negatively or positively through our own behaviours and the dialogue we speak.

Prepare your heart each morning and remind yourself how important it is to interact with people in a kind and courageous way. At the end of the day, do an honest assessment of how well you did. We can only change that which we recognize as needing to be changed. How we treat people says more about who we are than who they are. So take heed now and start preparing your heart so that your tongue is not sinking ships!

The Power to Own Your God-Given Vision Even If No One Else Can See It

"There have been moments in my life when every bone in my body has said, 'This is God at work—pay attention.'" —Rosita

Have you ever experienced a moment or a time in your life when you were so clear about an idea, a vision, or a direction for your life, but you were the only one who saw it or understood it? You couldn't really articulate it to others, but it was razor sharp in your mind. Every beat of your heart was saying, "*Yes*, this is it, you're on the right path, and this is exactly what you are supposed to be doing at this moment in time." That insight elicits such a powerful awareness and inspiration that it can be somewhat overwhelming. This is when you need to step back, take a deep breath in, and say a quiet prayer to God—he will lead you.

I am ever so grateful that I have been able to realize and embrace the vision that God has placed in my heart. I believe that God places that vision in each of us; some of us realize it sooner than others. The vision is connected to the gift he has given to each of us.

Sometimes if we are not careful, we will find ourselves detouring away from the direction God is leading us because we hit a bump in the road or a hurdle or two along the way. We assume that if God is directing the path, there should be no bumps or hurdles along the way, so in some cases we mistakenly search for a new path. Personally, I think the bumps in the road are just a part of the journey and maybe just God's way of saying, "Slow down."

I think we need to pay attention to the hurdles, recognize them for what they are, and work our way around them—if the vision we have is truly from God. These hurdles or bumps can be unexpected situations or circumstances that occur along the way that we see as a hindrance to our progress. The bumps can also be well-intentioned people who think they know what is best for us. If we are not careful, they will take us down a path that has absolutely nothing to do with the path that God is leading us down.

Fear can also be a hurdle or a stumbling block. It can keep us stagnant while we begin playing that old familiar tape of "I am not good enough; why would God equip me with such greatness?" But as Marianne Williamson has stated, "Our deepest fear is not that we are inadequate. Our deepest fear is that we are powerful beyond measure. It is our light, not our darkness that most frightens us." Yes, many of us are very afraid of the precious gift God has placed in each of our hearts.

I have found that it takes an intimate relationship with God, a concentration on his power and love, and a relentless determination to obey his word as our anchor when all the distractions attempt to steer us off course. We were made perfectly by a God who created us for his purpose, not the world's purpose. God gives us the vision, and it is up to us to give birth to it. There is no greater joy than to be walking in the light of our greatness or giftedness that is God given.

Imagine a world where we all walked in the light of who we were created to be. Where we focused on where

God needs us to be rather than where we think the world needs us to be. It takes an insurmountable amount of faith to walk to the beat of that which God has placed in our hearts, especially on those days when God steers us into what may appear to us as unknown territory. We must simply trust and stay true to the vision and God's love for us. If you have not already done so, make a commitment today to ask God for his vision for your life and for the courage to fulfill his vision and desire for your life. We all need to do our part in spreading light to the world. Stay with the vision—the time is now!

The Power of Silence

"No one has truly experienced 'silence' until one is able
to enter into his own inner sanctuary." –Rosita

Wow, I wonder how many of us reading this book right now would love to go to our inner sanctuary to escape all the external and internal noise that bombards us on a daily basis, and yes, the stress that comes with it? I don't know about you, but frankly my ears are screaming, "Stop!" I have had enough of all the external noise coming from roaring cars, roadside construction, TVs, cell phones, loud car stereos, and all the other sounds related to city living. Yes, I need to check back in with self. How about you? And not only do we have to be concerned about all of the external noise, but we also have a lot of internal ego-centric chatting going on inside of us. I would say we could all use some respite care.

Silence and stillness are ways of tapping into our inner sanctuary. We have, however, lived for so long in a state of busyness and noise that for some of us it is really hard to know how to be still and relax. The noise has become part of the norm. Even if we figure out a way to at least temporarily tune out the external noise, we often find it hard to tame the additional noise that comes from inside of us.

I was sitting with a group of women one evening, and one of them said she thinks people should go on "silence retreats" to get away from all the stress of daily living. Another woman spoke up and said, "I'd be afraid to do that; silence scares me." I think both she and many others are afraid of it because it has become so foreign; we are simply not used to it. We have all become so used to our frantic pace of life that silence unnerves us a bit, and when it is too quiet, we fill the space up with music or a TV show that we are not even listening to or watching. Let's face it, people, we are in some ways addicted to noise. Like any other addiction, there is always a price to pay. It is not healthy to be "on" 24/7; both the mind and body must be quieted.

I think the formula for tuning out the external noise might be a little easier than tuning out the chattering of our ego selves. This nonstop chatter fills our minds from the time we wake up in the morning until the time our head hits the pillow, and it continues on in the form of dreams or disruptive sleep patterns because we awaken to chattering involving thoughts or projects that unresolved or undone. We wander around in past moments that no longer belong to us, and we kill the joy of living in the present. We walk around uptight and stressed because we haven't spent enough time in that sanctuary of silence. Our busy jobs and family responsibilities involve nonstop noise and stimulation, but we can choose to tune out both the external and internal noise even if only for a few minutes a day. We will appreciate the impact those few moments of silence can bring to our lives in a positive way. Every day we should carve out time from our daily routines to sit quietly without any outside distractions and just appreciate the quietness. Silence is a way of reaching another part of our minds; it connects us to our source and our authentic power as well. It can remove tension and anxiety and help refuel our internal batteries. It can also help unleash our creative juices and the untapped greatness that often lies dormant.

Here are some suggestions to get you started on your journey of silence:

1. Take a few moments each morning to clear your mind. Breathe in and out. Be aware of each breath. Do this before you state your daily WRM intentions.

2. Keep your radio, television, computer, and cell phones off. Do not turn the cell phone on until after you've walked out the front door. The morning, prior to opening that front door, belongs to you.

3. Take an early morning walk before all the traffic and noise starts up in your neighbourhood.

4. Get up early and just sit in the quietness of your home before anyone else is up.

5. Find time in your day to meditate, and find prayer time to give thanks for all of your blessings.

6. Find time to sit in complete darkness in your home so you are not distracted by external stimuli, and enjoy who you are without all the noise and busyness.

The Power to Attract Light: A Carla in Your Life!

(*Carla* in Latin means strong one.)

I was determined that I was not going to join a small group at my church. I tried everything I possibly could to get out of yet another commitment that I knew I had no time for. But for some reason I found myself blurting out the words, "Yes, I will participate," and everything inside of me was saying, "Are you kidding me? You don't have time for this." Like most of you reading this book, I am over-committed. I quickly changed my mind and indicated that a Thursday night small group session was just not going to work for me. However, somehow I got talked into attending the first session and came home proclaiming to my husband that the group was not for me and, "Why is it that certain people think I should attend?"

Well, to make a long story short, I ended up going the following week as well, and before I knew it I was not only attending every session but participating with great enthusiasm. I actually looked forward to going every week. I was in a group of about six people. We ate supper together with a number of other small group participants, watched a video, and then went off to a room with our own small groups to discuss what we had learned. I had the privilege and pleasure of meeting a delightful woman by the name of Carla, and for some reason she and I clicked right away. We chatted for awhile about the connection we'd made, but neither of us knew why. I told her we should both go home and pray about it, and perhaps God would reveal what this connection was all about.

Have you ever met someone with whom you have felt an instant connection but were not really sure why? It was like I knew her from somewhere, as if we had met before.

I indeed went home and prayed about it. God kept revealing to me the word *light* and then *"light to light."* I thought, *Are we supposed to be light for each other, or was she sent to bring me light?* Now I was really intrigued. The next week I went back and told Carla my revelation. I asked if God had spoken to her about this connection, and she replied, "No, I didn't receive any great revelation." I joked with her and said, "Excuse me, but you need to do a little work on this too." She chuckled and said she'd get on it.

Each week as we attended session, we would greet each other by saying, "Light to light." Every once in awhile we would also send a Facebook message or an email encouraging each other, and there would always be reference to the light.

After the Thursday evening group sessions ended, I would see Carla at church on Sundays and we would greet each other with our light to light message. I believe that God purposely put Carla in my life and for a specific reason; perhaps even Carla doesn't know the reason. I am still trying to figure it out.

Carla has an abundance of energy. She is a gentle, humble, and kind spirit with an amazing sense of humour. I don't think she realizes the impact she has on others, which is probably why it is so amazing. Her presence is spirit driven and not ego driven.

Isn't it amazing how God just places people in our lives for the right reason and season? Perhaps Carla was sent to remind me that my cup needed filling and that in order for me to continue pouring out I needed to be poured into. I spend a large portion of my days encouraging and supporting individuals and groups through various challenges in the workplace. I think Carla was God's agent sent to remind me that God needed to pour into me that which he wanted me to pour out to others. Sometimes as speakers, social workers, or in any profession where we are in the helping, we forget about the pouring-into process. What I mean by that is taking the time needed to really connect with and understand the message God wants us to pour out to others. We can only do this if it is poured into us first; otherwise the message gets diluted and becomes our agenda for people instead of God's. If we let our ego take front stage, and not the heart of Christ Jesus, he will find a way to get us back on track again. In my case, he used Carla as his conduit to make this happen.

Carla has reminded me that we must all take time to dim the lights and get off the secular stage of life in order that we may spend some time alone reflecting, meditating, praying, evaluating, and listening to the messages and direction God has for our lives, that God is pouring into us.

Those Thursday evening sessions allowed me time to do just that.

God always knows the right people to place in your life, and at the right time. We don't need to know why; we just need to trust that God is on the job, paving the road that we will travel next. He cannot send us off on new paths to do his work if we are not carrying the rest message. We can only be fishers of men if we are carrying the right tools. The next time someone new comes into your life, remember my story with Carla and consider that perhaps they have been given an invitation from God to visit your heart and leave you a powerful message or vision.

The Power of a Fly High Posse!

"Success is not a solo act—we must choose carefully who will participate with us on our journey." —Rosita

As an entrepreneur, one of my greatest lessons has been that success attracts success. If you and I want to do great things, we must be around people who are doing great things. We need to be with people who will take us out of our place of average. I don't know about you, but I want to be around "fly high people." The best way to describe fly high people is that they are purpose driven: fearless, vivacious, focused, esteemed, bold, and hard-working, grace-filled achievers. They also think differently and can easily adapt to our ever-changing world. They do not buy into the concept of an idea being unrealistic. If they can imagine it, they go for it, and are usually quite successful.

The Wright brothers are an excellent example of this. They had an idea that most thought was laughable, but on December 17, 1903, after several years of secret work, they proved the naysayers wrong and their flying machine has since transformed the world. The lesson here is that success-driven fly high people keep moving forward even though others may label their idea unrealistic.

Finally, what I love the most about fly high people is that they are well disciplined and know that there is a force much bigger than all of us that enables us to do the extraordinary if we stay focused, work hard, and develop our skill set. In the words of Pastor T.D. Jakes, "No one trips across a finish line at the Olympics and says, 'Oh, wow! How did I do that?'" Rather, they accomplish something great because they diligently prepared themselves on a daily basis for years. As stated earlier, when preparation meets our giftedness, we become unstoppable. Align yourself with powerful people who can contribute to your growth. You don't get in life what you want, you get what you are. To become better, you need to hang around people who are doing better things than you are. If you are the smartest one amongst your friends, look for a new set of friends. This doesn't mean you have to get rid of your old group; you just need to expand your horizons. If you want success bad enough, then you are the only one who can create it.

I would suggest that you have a picture of what that success looks like to you. Orville and Wilbur Wright were visionaries, which is why they had remarkable success. You too must become a visionary and imagine what could be. If you know what you are striving to achieve and if you are aligning your thoughts, actions, and the words that you speak in that direction, you will attract the right people and resources in your life. The truth of the matter is that successful people are attracted to other successful people. If you're truly walking in your greatness, other people who are on the same path will find you. Wake up each day with a good attitude and a solution-oriented mindset, look for the good in people, and be sure you are well rested and ready to tap into the abundance that will come your way. Remember, when preparation meets greatness amazing things can happen. So, are you prepared?

Take this little test now by answering these questions:

1. What does success look like or mean to you? Success can be very subjective.

2. What are my short- and long-term plans to achieve my success goals?

3. Who do I have in my close circle of friends, and how are they supporting or hindering my ability to achieve my goals?

4. Do I have people outside of my circle of friends (mentors, coaches) who can assist me in achieving my success goals?

5. Is there anyone else who may be hampering my success? If so, what do I need to do to ensure that they don't?

6. Is it difficult for me to reach out and have conversations with other people about their success?

7. What actions can I take right now in order that I might begin the process of hanging with some fly high people who can inspire me to achieve my own success?

Remember, anything you can imagine is possible. Believe in yourself. Believe in the power of others who are always willing to help you if they know you are sincere and passionate about your goals. Now get going and create success your way! What you want to be tomorrow you have to do today!

The Power of the H.E.E.L.S.

"The higher the H.E.E.L.S., the greater the impact." —Rosita

What is it about women and their heels? We love our flats, lower heels, and runners, but there is something about the *high* stiletto heels that brings a woman to life, even if she only wears them for five minutes. I think it was Oprah who coined the term, "five-minute shoes." She said that every woman should own at least one pair, even if she can only wear them long enough to walk into an event and make a statement; when she sits down she can take them off. I have heeded Oprah's advice on several occasions. I am always fascinated by how women, including myself, can salivate over a pair of new stylish high heels. It appears as though heels can elevate both our altitude and our attitude. High heels have a way of making us all appear slimmer and more empowered. It amazes me at what a few inches on a pair of shoes can do for a woman's confidence.

On a personal note, I like to see the power of the heel in a different light. Here is my acronym for H.E.E.L.S.:

Honouring
Elevating
Encouraging

Loving
Strengthening

When we get up in the morning and put on our favourite pair of empowering heels, let's remember this acronym with each step that we take. Let it be a reminder that we have a responsibility to ensure that we walk with grace and compassion with everyone we come into contact with. We can do this by ensuring that our actions, behaviours, and interactions are always honouring, elevating, encouraging, loving, and strengthening the heart, soul, and mind of every woman we meet. That truly is the real power of the H.E.E.L.S.!

A Final Thought...

We live in a fast-paced world that can often times become overwhelming and exhausting. We struggle daily to find a cure to our insomnia, our overworked bodies, and our long to-do lists. We often don't recognize or take the time to realize that we are just one choice away from the life we truly want to live. I hope I have inspired you to think about the choices you make each day and that you really can live the life you deserve. Make a choice today that you will start applying some of the tips I've shared with you. This is my gift to you—open it, use it, and share it with others. *You've Got the Power!*

For more information, please visit:
www.rositahall.com

www.ingramcontent.com/pod-product-compliance
Lightning Source LLC
Chambersburg PA
CBHW072004090426
42740CB00011B/2077